D0053782

DECIDING WHO LEADS

DECIDING WHO LEADS

How Executive Recruiters Drive, Direct & Disrupt the Global Search for Leadership Talent

JOSEPH DANIEL McCOOL

Foreword by John A. Byrne, Executive Editor, *BusinessWeek*

Davies-Black Publishing
Mountain View, California

Published by Davies-Black Publishing, a division of CPP, Inc., 1055 Joaquin Road, 2nd Floor, Mountain View, CA 94043; 800-624-1765.

Special discounts on bulk quantities of Davies-Black books are available to corporations, professional associations, and other organizations. For details, contact the Director of Marketing and Sales at Davies-Black Publishing: 650-691-9123; fax 650-623-9271.

Visit the Davies-Black Publishing Web site at www.daviesblack.com.

Printed in the United States of America.
12 11 10 09 08 10 9 8 7 6 5 4 3 2 1

Library of Congress Cataloging-in-Publication Data
McCool, Joseph Daniel
Deciding who leads : how executive recruiters drive, direct, and disrupt the global search for leadership talent / Joseph Daniel McCool.—1st ed.
p. cm.
Includes bibliographical references and index.
ISBN 978-0-89106-246-2 (hardcover)
1. Executives—Recruiting. 2. Executive search firms. 3. Management. I. Title.
HF5549.5.R44M387 2008
658.4'07111—dc22

2007038477

FIRST EDITION
First printing 2008

For the loves of my life,
Kris, Lindsay, Erin, Matthew, and Sean

And further dedicated to campaigns to convince employers
to pay hardworking people around the world a livable wage, especially
caretakers of those in need and educators of young children

CONTENTS

FOREWORD

John A. Byrne, Executive Editor, *BusinessWeek*

I have only a "quintessential headhunter" to blame for it. The "it" being my endless fascination for the mysterious executive search business that remains today a relatively puny part of global management consulting.

Nearly a quarter century ago, I met my first executive search consultant—one of the world's best and best known. He had just completed one of the most celebrated searches ever, finding a chief executive for an extraordinary entrepreneur by the name of Steve Jobs at a fledgling company called Apple Computer. And I was dispatched to report and craft a profile for *Forbes* magazine.

When I walked through the doors of his search firm's modern offices on Park Avenue in New York, I was prepared for the expected charm offensive. But it didn't take long for this skeptical reporter to be won over. The man himself arrived with a generous smile, a firm handshake, and the self-confidence that comes to those at the top of their game. He regaled me with tales of success and failure, of his behind-the-curtain role as matchmaker in dozens of high-profile CEO searches, of his humble beginnings, of his belief that nothing was more important in business than leadership.

He was urbane, witty, thoughtful, even spiritual—the quintessential people person. He asked you about your own personal journey, your upbringing, your family, your goals, and your dreams. He took you into his confidence, and it was a comfortable place to be. His powers of observation were acute. All these years later, I still remember that he noted the cut and styling of my well-pressed Brooks Brothers suit, as if he was building my ego as a candidate for some future search assignment.

Not surprisingly, I wrote a fairly positive story—my first of many on the business of executive search consulting and the people engaged in it. That first, formative interview with the gregarious Jerry Roche led me to think that it would be easy work to meet many other fun-loving, high-spirited executive search characters, and so I jumped at the chance to write a book about this fascinating world. Published two years later, in 1986, *The Headhunters* became something of a cult classic among the hunted and the hunters. The book gained a worldwide audience, with far more impact than I ever imagined. Even today, I meet people who tell me they not merely read the book—they were inspired to make bold choices in their professional lives. Many left their corporate jobs to become executive search consultants.

So it is with delight and much satisfaction that I read the work of another journalist, far more knowledgeable than I about executive search, who has chosen to take this first deep dive in twenty-two years into a fascinating and critical business. The result, *Deciding Who Leads* by Joseph Daniel McCool, is in your hands. It is an impressive work, based on interviews with many in and outside the business and on Joe's own experiences, including his eight years as editor of *Executive Recruiter News.* The book also draws on Joe's most recent work as a writer and worldwide lecturer, and advocate for executive recruiting best practices.

This book could not have arrived at a more opportune moment. We live in a world that would greatly benefit from strong and smart leadership in all our companies, organizations, and governments.

As *Deciding Who Leads* so clearly details, what great leaders do is give purpose and direction to endeavor. They see a path ahead, a way to move forward, and they mobilize the people and the resources necessary for meaningful accomplishment. They inspire. They make magic happen. Anyone who has ever been fortunate to work for an authentic leader knows this in his or her bones. Great leadership is no small task in a world as truly complicated as the one in which we now live. Competition is fierce. Interests are divergent. Self-interest is the predominant mind-set.

And we have clearly seen the result of bad and ineffective leadership—something that is always in evidence. We've seen too many executives who are ambitious for themselves and not their companies or their people. We've seen too many executives who have abused their power and influence, who have violated our sense of ethics, of integrity, of values. And we have seen far too many executives who are charlatans, who lack the brains, the energy, the desire to truly lead.

Joe McCool takes us behind the scenes of executive search and reveals that what the best executive search consultants do is find and deliver extraordinary leadership talent. And no less crucial, they help make the connections that keep bad and ineffective people out of power. Of course, as *Deciding Who Leads* also details, it doesn't always work that way. Joe reveals the miscalculations, misfits, and mistakes of executive search. Few matches are perfect, and Joe gives us the good, the bad, the ugly, and the uglier. Best of all, he describes what the executive search world needs to do to live up to its awesome responsibilities—and what hiring organizations who engage executive search consultants need to do to improve their relationship and the results of leadership recruiting.

More often than not, executive search consulting is a business that gets it right—it's why executive recruiting has emerged into a much more significant and influential profession than it was when I first delved into it all those years ago. Thanks to Joe McCool for this insightful "insider" look at where the business stands today and where it needs to go in the future. Enjoy!

ACKNOWLEDGMENTS

When I first decided to move my career as a general assignment journalist toward a specialty focus on executive recruiting and management succession, I struggled with the notion that my days covering the news and events of my adopted home state of New Hampshire—including its first-in-the-nation presidential primary campaigns—were coming to an end. The voters of New Hampshire have long been tasked with the special civic duty of deciding who leads (and who shouldn't go any farther) after their primary, and it was a privilege to see that extraordinary leadership selection process unfold.

What I didn't then realize was that I was about to embark on a global educational journey that would give me a front-row seat from which to watch the corporate competition for leadership advantage unfold—a largely stealth pursuit driven, directed, and regularly disrupted by executive search consultants.

Over the course of the past decade, I've developed an intense interest in how the work of executive recruiters—widely misunderstood by many institutions and business leaders who engage their services—influences and alters the course of organizational performance, culture, and profits, and also makes or breaks the careers of tens of thousands of executives around the world each year. I've also developed a passion for sharing what I've learned from the masters of executive search consulting, as well as from corporate human resources, leadership staffing, and talent acquisition and management executives who are witness to the high-stakes drama, the victories and missteps that characterize today's executive search process and what is becoming an intense, truly global competition for leadership advantage.

I am indebted to many people for giving me the opportunity to take this incredible journey and to share those learnings in the pages of this book.

I am especially thankful to the many friends, colleagues, teachers, employers, mentors, and others who, over the past forty years, have presented me with opportunities to learn, develop, and grow, not only as a journalist and a business professional, but as a person, too.

I thank my friends from around the world and from across New Hampshire and the United States, from ExecuNet, *Search-Consult,* Plymouth State University, Gonzaga University, Kennedy Information, and Saint Patrick School, and from the world's most enjoyable early-morning ice hockey league, for their encouragement, advice, teaching, support, and friendship. And I would be remiss if I didn't thank the late James H. Kennedy III (1924–2006), the "conscience of the executive search profession," who provided my very first lessons about executive search consulting and its tremendous influence on organizations and people.

I am privileged to know and thankful for the guidance offered me by distinguished executive search consultants and business leaders on every continent, who have sharpened my perspective on their global work, including the executive recruiters and corporate executives who generously responded to my requests to contribute their time and insight to this book.

I would like to thank Laura Lawson, Laura Simonds, Lee Langhammer Law, Jill Anderson-Wilson, and the entire Davies-Black team for their support and encouragement, including Connie Kallback, who demonstrated amazing patience, concern, and friendship toward this first-time author through the publishing process.

I also want to thank and acknowledge the incredible blessing that is my family, without whose support, love, and inspiration this book could never have been written.

ABOUT THE AUTHOR

Joseph Daniel McCool is a writer, speaker, and consultant on executive search best practices and corporate management succession. He is also a senior contributing editor for ExecuNet, a leading executive career, business, and recruiting network; the featured columnist for *Search-Consult,* the international executive search magazine; and a contributor to *BusinessWeek* and other recruiting and management media.

Over the past decade, he has become the world's most widely quoted analyst of the global business of executive search consulting and its role in management succession. He has appeared on CNBC, has been interviewed on the CNN Radio Network, and has been quoted in news stories published by the *Financial Times, BusinessWeek,* the *Wall Street Journal,* the *Economist, Fortune,* Reuters, the *Los Angeles Times, Inc.* magazine, the *New York Times,* the *Globe and Mail of Toronto, Corporate Boardmember, Fast Company,* and *Investor's Business Daily.* He has also been cited or quoted as an expert on the executive search consulting business in three books, *The Road to CEO* (2000), *Executive Resource Management* (2000), and *Insider's Guide to Finding a Job* (2004).

He has been a frequent and repeat guest or keynote speaker at conferences addressing issues of executive search, management succession, and corporate recruiting best practices around the world. He has also written on leadership recruiting issues for *European CEO, Healthcare Executive,* and the *Industry Standard.*

McCool is the former editor in chief of *Executive Recruiter News (ERN),* which has provided insight, analysis, data, and opinion on the global executive search consulting business since 1980. During his eight-year tenure with *ERN*'s publisher, Kennedy Information Inc., a subsidiary of the Bureau of National Affairs Inc., he created and hosted the Executive Search Summit held annually in New York City from 2001 through 2005. He also edited the corporate and international editions of *The Directory of Executive Recruiters,* widely respected resources for companies and hiring executives wishing to select and engage executive search consultants. In addition, he authored a market research report titled *Executive Recruiting: Fees, Compensation and Key Operating Benchmarks* and served as a vice president with Kennedy Information Inc.

Before his work tracking the executive search business, McCool worked full time as a New Hampshire–based freelance contributor to the *New York Times* and correspondent for media in New England and across the United States, including United Press International, New Hampshire Public Radio, the *Boston Herald,* the *Union Leader and New Hampshire Sunday News,* and the *Washington Times.*

McCool holds a master's degree in organizational leadership from Gonzaga University and a bachelor's degree in business administration from Plymouth State College.

INTRODUCTION

Leadership recruiting and succession rank as the most pivotal agendas for today's growth-minded, change-oriented organizations. Given the risks and rewards inherent in senior-management recruiting, deciding who leads is the quintessential challenge faced by boards of directors, senior corporate officers, and division or line managers around the world. Their organizations' futures are cast in the investments they make—or fail to make—in leadership recruiting, development, and retention.

Human capital is, after all, the most critical intangible asset riding on corporate balance sheets, and executive recruiters occupy a unique brokerage position from which to drive, direct, and disrupt the global search for leadership talent.

THE INVISIBLE FORCE

With the demands of leadership at an all-time high and executive tenure at a record low, executive search consulting is the single most influential form of management consulting engaged by organizations. Working out of sight of public scrutiny, executive search consultants are an invisible force at the center of the global competition for the best leadership. They quietly influence executive compensation, management turnover, leadership development, and even employers' definitions of leadership. This at a time when these topics are increasingly the subject of media reports, shareholder meetings, and the everyday concerns of consumers, employees, academics, consultants, managers, and social researchers. These consultants' experience, networks, opinions, gut judgments, and, yes, biases collectively set the course and usually preordain the outcome of a search for leadership advantage.

Executive search consulting has been described by more than one of its practitioners as "the ultimate consulting business," and the truth is that no other professional services business has anywhere near its multibillion-dollar global impact on organizational performance, culture, and profits. Search consultants regularly move the financial markets when they recruit talented people to high-profile corporate leadership positions, and they similarly depreciate shareholder value when they lure a top executive away from an employer or when they accelerate or facilitate the exodus of key executives from a troubled company.

AGENTS OF CREATIVE AND DESTRUCTIVE INFLUENCE

So how should we judge those whose judgments so invisibly and routinely alter the course of global business? By virtue of their core matchmaking purpose, their track records, their own operating styles, and hiring organizations' widespread lack of sophistication when it comes to engaging them, executive search consultants are cast as both heroes and villains.

If decisions about people were easy and if these most influential of management consultants brought universal credibility and absolute consistency, theirs would be a widely understood and much-celebrated element of modern-day business building. But that's not the case. Executive recruiters orchestrate a mutual commitment process that is both art and science, and all parties to it must recognize that it is imperfect—as is all human behavior.

Executive search consultants are most appreciated when they serve as talent Sherpas—trusted knowledge leaders guiding hiring organizations through the unfamiliar and difficult terrain of the global market for leadership talent. They are most despised when they recruit key executives out of organizations that desperately need them—and when they make an imperfect judgment about an imperfect executive who turns out to be a misfit with the hiring organization.

The executive search profession summons people of great ambition who find professional fulfillment—and remarkable fortunes—in assessing a critical management or business challenge and then identifying, courting, and eventually persuading exceptional people to answer that call. Over time, executive search consultants can help hiring organizations achieve a strategic leadership advantage over their competition.

They discreetly facilitate a gradual commitment process between hiring organizations and proven business leaders, with all parties focused on how its eventual consummation will drive organizational performance. Executive recruiters infuse organizations with new leadership assets, and the best of them become trusted advisers to management with incredible insider access and unparalleled external influence over the course of organizational trajectory.

However, the true potential of executive recruiters' work can only be realized if hiring organizations become smarter consumers of their services, and if individual executives engage them always for the good of the companies they steward—not to smooth the path for their own next career move.

A LOOK BEHIND THE CURTAIN

This book raises the curtain on the challenges, agents, influence, and true potential of executive search consulting. It explores the growth, success, and wide acceptance of externally led executive management recruiting as well as the nagging obstacles it faces and the missed opportunities on its record.

This journey behind the scenes starts in Chapter 1 with a look at the global war for executive talent and the emerging market dynamics that are increasing expectations for the performance of corporate leadership at a time when executive tenure is in serious decline. Chapter 2 examines the end of management succession and executive recruiting as they've been known, and why organizations must improve on the status quo.

Chapter 3 examines leadership at Disney, a fascinating case study that offers an unprecedented revelation of one company's approach to CEO succession. Chapter 4 follows the trail of the "headhunters" as it leads to some paradoxical challenges, and explores the real identity problem facing those who facilitate the senior management succession process.

Chapter 5 explores the key ingredients that may come to define both the challenge to executive leadership and its solutions. This discussion is followed, in Chapter 6, by an accounting of the true cost of a bad executive hire, in which the direct costs—double or triple that individual's annual salary—account for only 20 percent of the total damage to the organization's performance.

Chapter 7 addresses the intersection of executive search and executive onboarding, an issue that hiring organizations must understand to hedge their sizable bets on leadership talent. These days, executives should expect well-planned support as they begin to tackle the challenges of a new senior management position. Chapter 8 speaks to the need for executive search consultants and those involved internally as parties to the executive search process to increase and improve their collaboration and demonstrate the impact of effective leadership recruiting.

Those who truly understand the influence of leadership recruiters will relate to Chapter 9, which discusses executive search as the key to leadership diversity, and others will begin to realize the magnitude of their consultant selection decisions by reading in Chapter 10 about how to engage executive search consultants.

The final chapter returns to the question of deciding who leads, examining best practices for senior management recruiting, and is intended to identify strategic priorities for hiring organizations as well as tactical advice for making the most of executive leadership recruiting and management succession.

1

THE GLOBAL WAR FOR EXECUTIVE TALENT

> No matter how good or how successful you are, or how clever or crafty, your business and its future are in the hands of the people you hire.
>
> **AKIO MORITA, FOUNDER, SONY CORPORATION[1]**

Deciding who leads is the most important challenge of our times for organizations the world over because the recruitment of senior executive management has the greatest bearing on the change that drives their financial performance. Executive search consultants, often called "headhunters," are the ones who make it happen because organizations frequently turn to them to find new leadership.

This decision is especially consequential because senior executives, more than any other employees, knit the fabric of employer culture into a coherent whole, mold the strategy that drives shareholder value, and set the rules that ultimately dictate the customer experience. They also sit in judgment about the kind of leaders who should be promoted or recruited into their ranks, thereby extending their imprint on the business and creating their professional legacy.

Today's leaders require meaningful experience, sound judgment, a moral compass, and a strategic vision to meet the challenges presented by external variables such as customer satisfaction and retention, corporate social responsibility, government regulation, and, increasingly, media and investor calls for governance and ethics reform, among others. Those who would lead must be adept at handling the organizational challenges over which they can assert significant control: growing net income; charting management succession; ensuring employee health, safety, and engagement; building relations with workers' unions; protecting the data privacy rights of consumers, employees, and recruits; growing the business; and generating and sustaining an acceptable long-term financial return to shareholders. The most visible leadership positions in any organization also create new role models as well as an effective platform from which to attract new talent.

All these factors may explain why the former treasurer of a major oil company who moved on to a career in the executive search business describes senior management talent as "the new oil . . . hard to find, difficult to extract and difficult to deliver."[2]

Whenever a key executive leaves, the company experiences a multiplier effect as other key contributors—including, invariably, others within the departed executive's trusted inner circle—leave or plan to depart ahead of the appointment of their boss's successor, who may come with plans to build and recruit a new cadre of trusted lieutenants and outside advisers.

The cumulative effect of senior leaders' decisions will either elevate corporate performance or inhibit profit growth, degrade organizational culture, and dissuade the best and most promising senior management candidates from staying or accepting a position there. But the increasing pressure to make smart, informed, and sometimes very public decisions and to embrace or adapt to the current business environment faster than the competition has put senior leaders under a microscope. The constant demands of executive management make it easy to understand why executives want to be paid so much for sacrificing their life outside work, even if the record sums they demand seem outlandish to observers.

Senior management talent is the new oil: hard to find, difficult to extract, and difficult to deliver.

TALENT AS "CEO SPEAK"

Walk into a room full of businesspeople these days and it won't take long to discover who among them hold the title of chief executive officer. They're the ones chatting about how important their best people are to their company's success. Whispering in one another's ears that they constantly worry about their best people being recruited away to the competition. Telling others that organizations that put people first finish first. Insisting that world-class management leadership helps drive competitive advantage.

Watch almost any television interview of a CEO or other leader, and invariably you'll see the interviewee bring the conversation around to the idea that people drive innovation, and that innovation and hard work drive performance and profits. As one says, "Physical capital depreciates, human capital appreciates." Also consider the words of the forty-first president of the United States, George Herbert Walker Bush: "Get good people, delegate and give 'em credit."[3] And this from former management consultant and Massachusetts governor Mitt Romney: "The key to good management is hiring the right people and building the best team."[4]

Often the CEO makes "talent" and "getting the right people in the right jobs" the cornerstone of a corporate transformation plan, as McDonald's CEO Jim Skinner did when he took the reins in December 2004. One informal poll of corporate HR managers revealed that 88 percent of them were employed by a company whose CEO had said people are the organization's most important asset.[5]

But setting the course for organizational change, or even simply inspiring others to follow, requires more than words from the CEO. It's true that you can't acquire the mantle of corporate leadership without saying the right things—and competing with world-class talent is indisputably one of the smartest messages a CEO can trumpet—but the vision and message have to be supported and implemented across the organization. So smart leaders have communicated that talent—specifically, the business of recruiting outstanding talent—is everyone's job.

"I talk about and think about people and succession every single day . . . we lead with people," says Susan Q. Hood, a vice president with the State Farm Insurance Companies. "Succession and developing people probably is my number one important work when I look at all the things I do."[6]

Radio advertisements for Saturn Corporation, the automobile manufacturer, tout its "People First" focus, which differentiates the company through its unique customer experience and employment proposition.[7]

Bloomberg, a global provider of data, news, and analytics, has invited talented individuals to consider its employment opportunities by emphasizing that "Our strength lies with our people."[8] Such messages about people and effective management—intended for both internal and external audiences—paired with the example and vision provided by the CEO and other leaders, will ultimately determine whether a company becomes a talent magnet, giving it a recruiting and employee retention advantage over the competition, or a hunting preserve, rendering it vulnerable to constantly being raided by the competition for its best talent, thereby inhibiting its growth.

But effective recruiting and management succession are two critical performance competencies precious few business leaders believe their organization has mastered. This may help explain why CEOs and other business leaders—including those who are only paying lip service to the talent issue—do so much talking about people, the workforce, and executive management. It also explains, in large part, why so many organizations have turned to business function outsourcing to bridge the talent gap.

Maybe hearing themselves say that their organization wins with its people makes CEOs feel better about their organization's current state of affairs. They may hope that merely saying the right things will add some level of support or sophistication to their often ineffective recruiting process and underdeveloped management succession plan.

A GLOBAL CHALLENGE

The business of senior management recruiting changes everything. That's because authority over the vast resources of today's enterprises—financial capital, political capital, and human capital—often gives those in positions of power inordinate control over the destiny of an organization and the wealth, careers, and lives of a multitude of others who are influenced by their decisions.

It has become increasingly clear that the victors in the war for executive recruitment, development, and retention will win in the global marketplace. The multinational companies and national economies of our world are moving toward a more congruous, interdependent, and competitive global economy that draws on the skills and experience of knowledge workers wherever they—and the brightest market opportunities—reside.

The truth is that we are all global consumers. Just think of the clothes you wear, the car you drive, the home electronics you use, and the goods you consume in the course of a day. No matter where you live, you likely own more internationally manufactured products than your parents did, and your children are exposed to more global products than you were at their age.

The victors in the war for executive recruitment, development, and retention will win in the global marketplace.

We are also global citizens. And we're all part of a global talent market, one that places a significant premium on talented senior executives. The challenge for senior executives is to inspire, challenge, and lead people so that, no matter where they work and live, they want to compete and win as part of an organization that adds purpose and a sense of personal growth to their work life.

The globalization of multinational companies largely results from their realization that the most promising consumer markets are found in the world's most populous nations, or in regions where governments, geographies, social customs, or cultural norms previously prevented such business expansion. Globalization is also the result of mergers and acquisitions and industry consolidation, driven partly by powerful forces outside the United States and Europe that are changing the complexion and the rules of engagement for many businesses.

"You are no longer competing just with the guy down the street, but also with people around the world."[9] That's what IBM senior vice president Robert Moffat said in an interview with the *New York Times* about his company's decision to hire fourteen thousand new workers in India and lay off up to thirteen thousand workers in Europe and the United States.

As workforces and consumer markets become more global and service businesses proliferate, CEOs worry about their ability to keep their scattered workforces nimble and strategically aligned to both the opportunities and the threats that arise from the global marketplace. The pressure to optimize workforce alignment requires the movement of management assets and forces executives to think at least two moves ahead when it comes to deploying talented business leaders. "We have to be able to put bright talent and expertise where there's a need . . . we need to be able to move the talent around," says one corporate executive.

You are no longer competing just with the guy down the street but also with people around the world.

The need to drive business on an international scale dictates the effective deployment of management talent inasmuch as it requires companies to talk to their customers, employees, and shareholders on a global scale. Consider the case of Mexican cement industry giant Cemex (NYSE: CX), which found that it had to translate its Web site into eighteen different languages, in part because it operates in fifty countries around the world.

The capacity to conduct business globally rests on individuals' willingness to follow opportunity and adapt to a new environment, much in the same way a German executive recently followed opportunity all the way to Shanghai, a new crossroads for international business. His sense of discovery was short-lived as he walked into a conference center there, to be greeted by a gathering of more than five thousand of his countrymen. These days opportunity attracts leaders like a magnet, no matter what the longitude and latitude.

Cases in Point

To gauge the globalization of business, consider the story of Avery Dennison Corporation. Founded in 1935 and based in Pasadena, California, Avery Dennison is a global leader in pressure-sensitive technology and innovative self-adhesive solutions for consumer products and label materials. It operates more than two hundred facilities worldwide that manufacture products sold in eighty-nine countries for the office, school, and home under the Avery brand. It also manufactures pressure-sensitive base materials, reflective and graphic materials, and performance polymers under the Fasson brand. And its retail information services unit provides retail and apparel manufacturing industries with a variety of price-marking and brand identification products. Avery Dennison's other businesses produce postage stamps, battery labels, and performance films, as well as a variety of specialty tapes.[10]

The company tapped into a significant market in the United States over the years, but the lion's share of its recent growth has come from other markets. The makeup of its annual sales—as well as its overall workforce—has shifted significantly, as Table 1 explains.

Avery Dennison has been recognized by both the Human Resource Planning Society and the HR consulting firm Hewitt Associates as one of the top twenty U.S. companies for leaders. J. Terry Schuler, its senior vice president of human resources, says the company's challenge now rests on building global leaders and global teams that can serve in any function, in any geography, and at any time.[11]

Avery Dennison is not alone in seeing its business and its workforce globalize—and in the process awakening to new challenges across its business lines and around the world. Microsoft, for example, recruits about 25 percent of its top executives from external sources, and, as with many growing multinational companies, an increasing number

TABLE 1 **Avery Dennison: From Feudal Society to Global Company**

	1995	2006
Sales Non-U.S. Sales	$3.1 billion 40%	$5.7 billion 59%
Employees Non-U.S. Employees	15,500 35%	22,600 69%
Business model	• Small, autonomous business units • Highly decentralized • Margin, cost driven • Very few common systems, processes, tools	• Larger regional and global units • Marketplace decentralized, shared back office • Growth, productivity, and people goals • Common systems, processes, tools
Leadership development	• Low priority • Highly decentralized • No shared tools, processes • No formal development programs • Managers not held accountable	• High priority • Corporate driven • Common tools, processes • Formal development programs • Managers measured and held accountable

Source: J. Terry Schuler, Avery Dennison's SVP of HR, "High-Potential Career Development: Creating the Right Opportunities for Growth," presentation to The Conference Board Succession Management Conference in Chicago, October 26, 2006.

of its employees and senior managers work in and are citizens of countries other than the United States. The company also assesses the performance of its senior executives based partly on how effectively they attract and develop talent, which is key to Microsoft's ability to innovate and serve its customers' needs.[12]

That kind of thinking is shaping corporate attitudes around the world, as it did when the Corporate Executive Board, a provider of business research and executive education programs in Washington, D.C., polled a global audience of senior HR managers. Three-quarters of those respondents indicated that "attracting and retaining" talent was their number one priority.[13]

The Coca-Cola Company has a significant thirst for superior global management leaders, and the competition for top executives that it faces in regional markets around the world suggests future growth for what has become a truly global market for leadership talent.

"We certainly are approaching this work with more of a global view," says John J. Goldberg, director of executive talent acquisition within the human resources function of The Coca-Cola Company.

> *We view things a little differently when we source talent globally, and that translates into how we do [executive] search. I don't think executive recruiting could be more critical in a company like ours. The Coca-Cola Company itself is only half the business, with a focus on brand development, marketing, quality, and strategy. Our bottling partners manufacture and sell our products. This leaves us with a workforce largely comprised of knowledge workers. The cliché about our people being our greatest asset rings true here, . . . and it is clearly an absolute priority of our leadership.*

Goldberg says Coke's sheer size and its need for management leaders dictate that the company employs a truly international workforce. "We do business in over 200 countries. For us to reflect our consumer base we have to have an extremely global team. We are competing for talent all over the globe."

Further, Goldberg says, the company values the flexibility its senior executives bring in because it wants to have options for deploying its executive-level assets—in part to expose its business leaders to challenges that may arise in any region of the world. "People are on their own growth paths," he says, citing a U.S. American running operations in Brazil and a Colombian running Coke's Asian business. "They are constantly on the move in their careers . . . we value mobility in our executives."

While many other executives have tackled the challenges presented by Coke's management-level vacancies, new job creation, and succession plan, Goldberg confirms that he is the first person within the company with exclusive responsibility for executive search. He says he spends at least 50 percent of his time recruiting executive talent outside the United States, and his many travels to Asia at times move that number closer to 70 percent. That's because of Coke's global talent needs and the opening of a truly global front in the war for leadership talent.

"There's greater visibility today as to where the talent is," he says, "but the work of senior-management recruiting has always been difficult. If you're seeking top management talent, you're always looking for a smaller piece of the [global workforce]."

And while he may be logging more frequent flyer miles than his talent acquisition peers in other companies, Goldberg says his travels outside the United States to recruit outstanding management talent make him a good fit with the company's other road warriors—all driving the performance of the world's largest beverage company with the most extensive distribution system in the world.

THE LEADERSHIP CRUNCH

The market for professional and management talent is cyclical, like the business cycle itself. During the late 1990s in the United States, for example, employers were paying handsomely and recruiting talented workers at a staggering pace. In the years since, the growth and contraction of industrial economies has moved large multinational companies to hire by the thousands and lay off by the thousands. The struggle for human capital has alternately cooled and re-ignited, ensnaring midsized, small, and now micro-companies in a battle for talent in economies far more reliant on their vitality as businesses.

We're only now in the opening skirmishes of the global war for executive talent. For organizations that find themselves unprepared to engage in it to defend their precious leadership assets, the truth hurts. It's painfully clear that all participants in this war need to make whatever succession plans they have more global and more inclusive.

These days, shifting demographics and a serious decrease in executive job tenure portend serious leadership succession challenges, and the implications of not planning for these challenges (or simply continuing to promulgate haphazard recruitment and retention practices that bring mixed results) will be far more punishing to corporate profits than in years past.

The fateful combination of demographic change and organizational dysfunction that has pushed executive turnover to new records in recent years has left the future of many fine organizations hanging in the balance. The graying of executive ranks, together with organizations' failure to develop management bench strength, has left many unable to provide internal replacements for the increasing numbers of top business leaders who will soon head into retirement. In fact, a study by RHR International, a U.S.-based human resources consultancy, found that 50 percent of the Fortune 500 companies anticipated losing half their senior management by 2008, while only about 25 percent were highly confident that their internal talent pool would meet the organization's future needs.[14]

Effective recruiting is a key to addressing those issues because, as global consulting firm Watson Wyatt has found, "organizations with superior recruiting practices . . . financially outperform those with less effective programs."[15] And research by Hewitt Associates, a global human resources company, found that "the attraction and retention of pivotal employees plays a critical role in increasing shareholder value."[16]

All of the following factors will combine to raise the stakes for leadership recruiting and retention:

- Significant demographic shifts
- Younger workers' demands for more work-life balance
- The unwillingness of many seasoned managers to relocate or accept foreign assignments. This is based in part on corporate

mishandling of other employees' returns and reintegration into their home country after such time away, lack of institutional memory of such sacrifices, and perhaps even the departure of the executive or HR leader who first advocated for the move overseas.

- Lack of exposure to more than one language and culture among many talented executives
- Companies' failure to retain Baby Boomers' institutional knowledge and develop meaningful succession management plans

The crunch will be especially acute at the senior management level. The future dearth of executive job candidates will result from a smaller pool of talent from which to draw replacements for retiring Baby Boomers, and it will pose a significant future challenge to corporate performance and economic output in most of the world's industrialized nations.

In light of the looming retirement of the Baby Boom generation, close to 40 percent of the HR executives whose views were cited in a 2006 report released jointly by Ernst & Young LLP, ExecuNet, and The Human Capital Institute indicated that their chief concern is the availability of talent over the next five years.[17] That finding prompted the survey organizers to raise a serious and as-yet-unanswered question: "Will corporate America move from productivity to 'reductivity'?"[18] The same question can be asked of other industrialized nations as well, especially those facing a significant drop in their birth rate.

Even for those companies with succession plans, talent management strategies, and executive development programs, those initiatives simply are not generating leaders fast enough to give organizations confidence that they're well prepared to meet their future challenges.

Many companies face the stark reality that a majority of their senior executives could retire *now*, and that their leadership bench strength is weak in some functions and business units. Others know that they've identified successors for only a small percentage of their most critical senior management jobs, and fewer have a strong grasp on which of their top leadership posts can be filled through internal promotion and which must be filled with new hires.

The competition for leadership talent will intensify as companies realize that replacing the productivity of one retiring Baby Boomer may require hiring more than one Generation Xer. And the interests of organizations and a new generation of executives wanting at least some work-life balance will soon collide. There simply may not be, from a productivity perspective, a clean one-for-one transfer of knowledge, experience, and productivity as the mantle of leadership is passed by the Baby Boomers to Gen X. This will only exacerbate the competition for the best leaders.

The mandate to lead increasingly global organizations, and companies' realization that they'll be unable to develop senior management talent fast enough to keep pace with the challenges and competitive threats posed by the global marketplace, will lead many organizations to reexamine their approach to recruiting top executives.

There may not be a clean one-for-one transfer of knowledge, experience, and productivity from Baby Boomers to Gen X.

THE SEARCH FOR MANAGEMENT TALENT

More and more of the world's largest corporations are centralizing the executive staffing function, building not only their capacity to manage search firm relationships but also their capacity for sourcing (and, in some cases, directly recruiting) the most talented executives, no matter what time zone or organization they're now working in.

While other elements of the people side of business are outsourced, many leading global organizations have opted to retain responsibility for strategic executive hiring. Striking the right balance between developing senior management talent internally and recruiting from the outside to inject new blood, fresh perspectives, and positive change is no easy task.

Here are some key considerations that senior business leaders must assess before they set out to link good recruitment practices to organizational performance:

- What is the organization's employment brand? How would current employees describe its culture?
- Does the organization have a senior management succession plan and an effective scorecard against which to assess the performance of high-performers and high-potentials within its ranks?
- Does the organization have productive relationships with executive search firms that have no significant talent blockage issues and policies against recruiting people away from current or recent corporate clients?
- Has the organization hedged its bet on external hires with an effective executive onboarding process that provides newly hired managers with feedback to alert them to cultural or performance missteps before they are sacked?
- Is the workforce nimble, knowledge based, and aligned globally to competitive pressures and opportunities?

The answers to these questions separate organizations that lead with people and world-class executive leadership from those with growth plans that may be challenged in today's competitive and stressed business environment.

Campbell Soup Company sells its products—including those in the V8, Godiva, Prego, and Pepperidge Farm brands, and, of course, its signature line of Campbell's soups, a product with more than 140 years of brand heritage—in more than 120 countries around the world. When Douglas R. Conant, Campbell Soup's president and CEO, took the helm, he realized that the company wasn't reaching its full potential and that it wouldn't deliver the highest total shareholder value in the food industry unless it began a transformation plan.[19]

"You can't talk yourself out of a situation you behaved your way into, so you've got to behave your way out of it," Conant says. To attract the very best senior management talent, "You have to have a compelling proposition, and I have to say, it's about more than money.... You have to, as a leader, create a culture that goes far beyond the financial remuneration."

Conant has done lunch or dinner with "high performers in the food industry" at least twice a month for about twenty years, and he says those interactions have given him a "visceral understanding of talent." He and his company rely on external talent to fuel Campbell's strategic vision, and when it comes to recruiting high-caliber management talent, Conant does what many chief executives do: "You call your friends in the executive search business." Those friends helped Conant drive the corporate transformation plan that began to take shape in 2000 and was revealed on the front cover of the company's 2001 annual report in one simple statement: "It's not enough to be a legend."

In addition, executive recruiters helped revitalize and restock the ranks of the 350 senior management executives who were, at the start of that strategic renewal, members of Campbell's Global Leadership Team (GLT). A combination of promotions from within and executive recruiting from outside the company has positioned the company's top leadership for success. In 2000, Campbell had 350 people in the GLT. The number was the same in 2006—but only 50 of the names were carryovers from the earlier list. Of the remainder, 150 were promotions from within the company, and 150 had been recruited into the GLT from outside.[20]

OUTSIDE RECRUITING

Going outside the organization for exceptional talent can lend new vision, leadership, and energy to a senior management team, an operating unit, or the company as a whole, and so presents a rare opportunity to strengthen the organization, introduce change, and otherwise elevate corporate performance. Sometimes outside recruiting is the only choice for a company whose top executive has retired, died, decided to devote more time to family life, or been recruited away to the competition. In some cases, an organization may decide to launch a search to replace an underperforming or misfit executive it intends to fire as soon as a successor is found.

Executive search is often the only way hiring companies can attract and recruit the senior management talent they need. Consider the case of Boeing (NYSE: BA), the world's largest aerospace company, which lured W. James McNerney Jr. away from his post as chairman of the board and CEO at 3M because Boeing needed an outsider to win back investors' trust. McNerney had been a runner-up for the CEO job at General Electric, where he worked for nineteen years before joining 3M. General Electric has, over many years, earned a reputation for training and developing high-caliber leaders, and, as a result, its executives have been prime recruiting targets.

Corporate reliance on the external leadership talent market is critical to change management, performance improvement, and management succession. As one corporate vice president of global talent management puts it: "We're realizing we just can't continue to rely on [internal] talent. You're going to see us hiring more from the outside." Another big-business leader puts it this way: "Inbreeding can be a problem with promoting from within." Still another points out that "We have gotten hit with market changes we didn't see," and recruiting new senior management is an effective way of buying strong corporate leadership and critical market intelligence at the same time.

The business of picking new, world-class corporate leaders is not easy, and the search for game-changing talent is especially difficult. Just ask the owner of virtually any professional sports team about the first-round draft picks that never led their teams to the playoffs, let alone a single winning season. He or she will tell you that in addition to the most methodical and scholarly analysis, there's a measure of luck, timing, and maybe even karma involved. Much in the same way the draft is key to the success of professional sports teams, recruiting great talent is key to organizational performance in the business world.

Going outside the organization to conduct a search for new executive management can be a risky proposition for the corporation, the executive, and those directly involved in the recruiting. And if there's anything that rankles with shareholders, it's uncertainty, risk, and surprises that shake their confidence in senior management. Effective management succession and the process of effective and seamless executive recruiting are key to mitigating risk for the corporation.

EXECUTIVE RECRUITERS AT THE CROSSROADS

Executive career mobility is a signpost of a free market economy, and executive recruiters lubricate the process that moves executives across the secret market for corporate management. These recruiters, or "executive search consultants" as the most strategic among them prefer to be called, are the ones who collectively plan, orchestrate, and profit from executive career movement and corporate leadership transition.

Standing at the critical intersection of management succession, executive recruiters collectively facilitate more than one-third of all six-figure executive moves and more than three-fourths of the highest-profile CEO transitions around the world. Their consideration of internal management candidates as part of the "external search" process also drives and lends credibility to an enormous number of executive promotions each year. Executive recruiters are the people that CEOs and other business leaders turn to in times of growth, in times of crisis, and every day and nearly everywhere modern-day business is done—whenever the need for management talent demands the riches of the external leadership market and an outsider's informed judgment on management assessment and potential.

Recruiting leadership talent is critical, as the late Peter Drucker once wrote in the *Harvard Business Review:*

Executives spend more time on managing people and making people decisions than on anything else—and they should. No other decisions are so long lasting in their consequences or so difficult to make. And yet, by and large, executives make poor promotion and staffing decisions. By all accounts, their batting average is no better than .333: at most one-third of such decisions turn out right; one-third are minimally effective; and one-third are outright failures. In no other area of management would we put up with such miserable performance.[21]

Business leaders have come to know that executive recruiters can help them probe the external talent market and also see their own organization—its strengths, its warts, and its unique culture—from a different perspective. Business leaders also worry about losing key management talent, and thoughts of having their stars stolen by savvy recruiters can keep them up all night.

Executive search consultants are storytellers. They use their arts of persuasion, social graces, assignment-specific jargon, and people-reading skills to assess candidates' fit for the role and sell them on the employer's history, vision, and strategy. They are also masters of a covert craft that relies heavily on discretion and its practitioners' ability to see and communicate how an executive's gifts, experience, character, and vision can boost a corporate client's performance.

The serious business of senior management recruiting demands that businesses partner with more than a mere recruiter. Getting it right requires corporate partnership with experts in executive courtship and assessment and the consummation of a marriage of interests between hiring organization and candidate. It also demands more than just recruiting know-how. It requires recruiters who are also consultants capable of evaluating an organization's talent mapping to determine what external human assets may be needed. And that requires sufficient objectivity to decide when a need can be fulfilled through referrals and when an executive search firm is best positioned to drive the search for new leadership.

The executive search business has been a global enterprise since its emergence from the world's largest management consulting firms in the early twentieth century. Executive search consultants have led cross-border searches for decades, and given that experience, they are uniquely qualified to serve as international talent scouts for globally minded organizations.

Consider the case of the long-respected London-based search consultant who recruited a technology executive in Marin County, California, and placed him as the CEO of a software company in Budapest. Or the distinguished Auckland-based consultant whose search for a new country manager for a New York company led him to four short-list candidates: an American living in Germany, a British citizen living in London, an Indian residing in Bangkok, and a fellow New Zealander living in Sydney, all of whom were eventually introduced to the client during a meeting in Singapore. Or any of a host of American, European, Japanese, Brazilian, and Korean search consultants—and others working in every industrialized nation—who have recruited key executives for corporate clients many time zones removed from their offices.

For corporate employers who have operated entirely within the borders of their home country, says retired search consultant Leon Farley, former president of the Association of Executive Search Consultants, "The international sourcing of candidates is the next big challenge in executive search." The world will need more business leaders—and executive search consultants, for that matter—who are urbane, culturally sensitive, and skilled in multiple languages to recruit talented individuals around the world, he adds.

Executive search is a modern management tool and an essential component of corporate and not-for-profit management succession, and the executive search consultant has become a vital agent in leadership recruiting and executive opportunity spotting.

John Sculley, the former PepsiCo executive famously recruited to be CEO of Apple Computer by Steve Jobs's challenge, "Do you want to spend the rest of your life selling sugared water or do you want a chance to change the world?"[22] knows that to be true. The executive search consultant who choreographed this transition, Sculley told me in 2005, "was someone who was there as a trusted and valued person in that whole process."

Executive search consulting is a form of business consultancy with an especially bright future, in part, according to Harvard Business School professor Michael Watkins, because it feeds an appetite for leadership talent stoked by the Fortune 500 companies, where, he estimates, more than 500,000 management positions turn over each year.[23]

If done well, executive search consulting has no substitute. Emerging talent management and succession planning practices rely on it. So does the people side of business, where a high-performance team builds a high-performance culture that drives consistent results for shareholders. As one corporate executive has said, the external search for management leadership helps deliver the "frequent dosing of change" critical for companies that are now part of a global economy in which the concept of value and the demands of leadership are constantly being redefined.

If done well, executive search consulting has no substitute.

2

REENGINEERING EXECUTIVE SEARCH AND MANAGEMENT SUCCESSION

If we did our job [developing leaders], we'd never call you.

JACK WELCH, RETIRED CHAIRMAN AND CEO, GENERAL ELECTRIC[1]

The productivity, performance, and profitability of organizations worldwide can no longer be sustained in a global business environment that demands more out of leadership and effective change management while relying on an incredibly lackluster tradition of senior management succession and executive recruitment. The business of recruiting corporate leaders is especially serious because of how it influences the financial performance of organizations, returns on shareholder investment, and the careers and livelihoods of millions of professional and blue-collar employees (and by extension, their families and communities) around the world.

The mostly unwritten rules that have governed the way companies recruit their senior leadership have gone unchecked and unchanged for about ninety years, since the very first executive search consulting practices were conceived inside some of corporate America's burgeoning management consulting firms. That may explain why, today, executive tenure and public confidence in corporate management are at an all-time low while the demands of organizational leadership have never been higher.

The truth is that executive recruiters are both part of the problem and part of the solution. Because they drive, direct, and disrupt the global search for leadership advantage, they can be both builders and destroyers of organizational culture, earnings, teams, product delivery schedules, customer relationships, R&D, momentum, and succession plans. They shape the culture and performance trajectory of organizations as no other outside advisers to management can.

In my experience, executive search consultants recruit or are involved in as much as 35 percent of all new hires (as opposed to promotions) at a minimum $200,000 salary each year. They are engaged to lead or support slightly more than half of all the searches to replace CEOs and other "C-suite" executives at public companies around the world, and their influence over the makeup of private equity management continues to grow. Their work has enormous consequences, especially for people who either don't know about or don't understand the role these recruiters play and the effect they have on corporate leadership transitions.

Executive search consultants shape the culture and performance trajectory of organizations as no other outside advisers to management can.

The wholly unregulated global business (which generates $10 billion annually in professional fee revenue) has contributed to the wild escalation of senior executive compensation—to the point where, in 2005, according to a recent Economic Policy Institute study, the average CEO was paid 821 times as much as a minimum wage earner, who was earning just $5.15 per hour.[2] That CEO earned more before lunchtime on the first workday of the year than the minimum wage worker earned all year.

Executive recruiters have long shaped corporate employers' views of the supply-and-demand dynamics of the executive labor market because theirs are the voices, perspectives, experiences, and opinions of the free market economy. Their insights, coupled with their access to the external leadership talent, have enabled client hiring organizations to compete in that market. Recruiters are the silent vanguard—way out ahead of the Wall Street analysts—when it comes to judging corporate management performance and identifying employers of choice.

When an executive plans to leave an organization or aspires to join it, the executive recruiters are often the first to know. They know exactly what it takes to lure individual executives at outstanding organizations and how to persuade such talented performers—most of whom aren't looking for another job—to come and work for their client organizations. They know what's behind the exodus of key managers from underperforming and dysfunctional organizations and why they should be leaving. They know precisely how much one company paid to recruit a vice president of marketing from a competitor. And they can tell clients about another company's failure to sweeten its offer to land a sought-after executive, who ultimately rejected the overture.

What's more, these executive talent scouts find themselves in an especially influential role when it comes to either accelerating or deescalating the migration of executive talent. This has huge implications for corporate earnings.

In some of the clearest terms—those relating to executive pay—executive recruiters continually challenge conventional wisdom by convincing those most interested in luring the competition's best-performing executives that they'll have to step up and pay more to do it. Executive recruiters have a vested interest in selling the potential rewards of recruiting executives externally, and they've been particularly good at selling the "Superman" qualities of potential CEO recruits.

Generally speaking, they market organizational change and change agents because employers long ago came to terms with the fact that change is a necessary fuel for organizational growth, and also that they'd have to pay at least a 15 percent to 20 percent premium to recruit someone from the outside, presenting a significant income opportunity for those positioned as the lubricants and third-party facilitators of the executive labor market. And while executive recruiters have continually emphasized the value of change, thereby escalating executive compensation, they have concurrently inflated the amount of their fees—making theirs an especially profitable business exercise.

These market dynamics have often put internal candidates at a decided disadvantage, partly because they lack an external advocate and partly because executive recruiters have succeeded in convincing the top brass that they need to add something to stay ahead of or even keep up with the competition. In fact, the prospect of improving their organization's lot while weakening the competition has always attracted corporate chieftains to the idea of recruiting from the outside rather than promoting from the inside.

The best-known executive search consulting firms have, over the years and by virtue of their predilection for recruiting the alumni of Harvard, Yale, and highly regarded business schools, largely failed to bring diversity to the senior management ranks, despite being in a remarkable position to do just that. That's because their Rolodex files were, in years past, populated almost exclusively by the white, male, and middle-aged—the exclusive demographic group they would rub shoulders with at the country club, on the golf course, and in the boardroom. Today, their computerized candidate databases can include profiles on more than a million outstanding executives from around the world, but they are only slightly more inclusive of women and minorities than the old Rolodex files, and still heavily populated by the social and economic elite.

None of the world's five largest international executive search consulting firms (each counting global annual fee revenue of more than $430 million) has ever been led by a woman. In recent years, an increasing number of partner-level hires (and some of the profession's best) have been women. However, white males with "elite-school" pedigrees, friends in power, and limited lifetime exposure to those in different socioeconomic strata are still the mold for too many search firms.

Given those realities, it's really no wonder that the work of executive search consultants has helped to maintain the status quo and extend the power of the "good ol' boy" network. It is easier for search consultants to recruit someone who looks like the person who agreed to retain them (most often the CEO or a senior line or business unit executive) than to challenge the job specification (and risk losing the search assignment) by questioning whether the organization is sufficiently diverse.

In the consultants' defense, this failure to diversify is equally the failure of entrenched business leaders, who refuse to consider any candidate who hasn't already held the same title with another employer. This cycle feeds on itself, ensuring that few who aren't already in positions of authority will ever ascend to the corner office, or even get within sight of it.

UNREALIZED POTENTIAL

The real paradox in the work of executive search consultants is that while these consultants have presided over and choreographed an important business process that has them deciding which candidates to introduce to client employers, they've largely failed to fulfill the potential of playing such a critical role in deciding who leads. Instead, that process often confounds the people who are touched by it, alienates a fair number of those urged to consider moving from one company to another, and otherwise perpetuates long-standing negative perceptions of specialized executive talent brokers, even among the organizations and business leaders that retain them.

Much of the problem stems from one fact: Despite offering a service grounded in organizational change and based on locating leaders who can create positive change, executive search consultants the world over almost universally get an unsatisfactory grade for their unwillingness or inability to see why they, too, must change.

As it turns out, a reevaluation and realignment of corporate management succession and senior management recruiting would do considerable good for all involved. Corporate employers looking to retain a higher percentage of executives recruited from the outside have a significant vested interest. That's because a bad executive hire comes at the cost of a substantial multiple of first-year compensation, the dollar figure that serves as the basis for executive search consultants' fee calculations.

Many candidates who agree to engage in the executive talent assessment and selection process—and whom I have heard described as "contestants"—are confused about what they are getting into. That claim is supported by the view of one executive search insider, who says, "This industry is a mystery to most businesspeople." As a result, some bring inflated expectations to the process, while others become emotionally overinvested in it and thus risk doing their careers (and themselves) serious harm. These contestants will surely welcome any change that leaves them better informed about the executive search process and otherwise leads to their being treated with more dignity and humanity, especially when they're not included as a finalist in a search assignment.

Executive search consultants would also benefit from a reengineered executive recruitment process. Despite their personal relationships with those in the upper echelon of corporate leadership, their special access to the inner workings of the client organization, and their intimate knowledge of the interpersonal, human dynamics that drive it, they tend to be relegated to transaction broker status and fail to engage the CEO as a true business partner.

Many candidates . . . are confused about what they are getting into.

In addition, the shareholders and employees of organizations around the world—who have seen how making poor leadership selections has led companies into scandal and bankruptcy—will welcome any change that brings stability, continuity, and confidence in the process that identifies, integrates, develops, and retains the best senior corporate leaders.

There really is no other choice than to reassess and realign management succession and the business of recruiting executive talent.

THE SEARCH FOR LEADERSHIP ADVANTAGE

The demands of corporate leadership have escalated significantly in recent years. Globalization, environmental concerns, foreign competition, advances in technology and science, and demographic trends all combine to pressure organizations to innovate and differentiate constantly, tirelessly, and relentlessly.

Organizations today need leaders who are as emotionally intelligent as they are savvy about business. They need leaders who bring a sense of humility rather than a sense of entitlement to their work. They need leaders driven by a call to serve others and not by greed and self-gratification. And they need leaders with a global view and sensitivity to the world, if not actual global working experience, to serve an international customer base.

True leaders in today's world respect the need for both fair and fully disclosed corporate governance. They appreciate and understand the business case for creating a truly inclusive work environment, where people are recruited, developed, and promoted on the basis of their skills, knowledge, and abilities, not on their gender, skin color, religion, ethnic identity, sexual orientation, or any other personal differentiator. And, increasingly, they must understand how human capital, and especially leadership talent, defines, differentiates, and drives organizational performance. They must appreciate that the competition can copy their organization's strategy, process, and products, but not its people and their collective ability to innovate and invent.

But shouldn't all that's now expected of today's leaders also be expected of those who recruit them? Executive search consultants have no leadership litmus test. But with the growth and development of a new generation of senior management recruiters should come the expectation that those engaged in the business are the equal or better of those they are engaged to recruit, at least in terms of the new management requirements outlined above.

Corporate leaders who know the real value of outstanding executive talent know what their ability to recruit and retain the best and brightest does for their bottom line. They also have a vested interest in the quality and character of the individuals who serve as their eyes and ears in the global executive talent market.

"I've always had a love-hate relationship with the search industry," former General Electric CEO Jack Welch once told an audience of executive search consultants. "I'd like to put you all out of business. If we did our job [developing leaders], we'd never call you."[3]

The challenge for today's executive search consultant, as it has long been, is to build relationships with corporate employers by serving as their ambassador to potential six-figure-salaried recruits, and then to elevate those relationships to the point where the consultant won't be tempted to leverage the benefits of such privilege by recruiting people out of the organization.

The golden rule of executive search consulting—the self-policed practice of considering the senior management of a current or recent client off-limits for recruiting—has been under significant pressure over the past decade, and isn't even widely known to or understood by most corporate clients. That's part of the reason why so-called headhunters, despite the gravity of their work for clients, are perceived as mercenaries and transaction dealers by the surprisingly unsophisticated majority of corporate buyers of executive search consulting.

KNOWLEDGE LEADERS FOR DIFFICULT TERRAIN

Executive search consultants, in the best sense of their mission, purpose, and aspirations, are akin to mountain guides for their corporate clients. The rewards of executive recruiting excellence are undoubtedly worth the risks, but, as with the dangerous ascent of any Himalayan peak, experience matters and a single misstep can lead to disaster.

"By far the best proof is experience," the English author and philosopher Francis Bacon (1561–1626) said. And that's precisely why the experience, skill, and intuition of their guide for the journey that is the executive search process means so much to corporate employers.

Consider the case of the beekeeper from New Zealand who, on May 29, 1953, made history when he reached the summit of Mount Everest, the world's tallest peak, some 8,848 meters or 29,035 feet above sea level. Ever since, schoolchildren around the world have learned that Edmund Hillary, later dubbed Sir Edmund Hillary, was the first explorer to reach the top of the world. But Hillary wasn't alone.

History has been kind to the Kiwi known to many in his homeland simply as "Ed," who became a hero to native peoples throughout the Himalayas because of his work to build schools, hospitals, bridges, freshwater pipelines, medical clinics, and other badly needed frontier infrastructure. Far fewer people remember Sherpa Tenzing Norgay, who also topped Everest that day and without whom Hillary and the entire British mountaineering expedition might never have reached the roof of the world.

The British recruited Tenzing Norgay for a reason. He knew the challenge. He had been the guide on four previous Everest campaigns, and he knew the mountain like no other, having reached to within about eight hundred feet of the summit with a Swiss expedition in 1952.

One dictionary defines *Sherpa* as follows:

- A member of a Tibetan people living in the Nepalese Himalayas
- A knowledge leader familiar with unknown or difficult terrain
- One who leads

Those definitions describe and do justice to the world's leading executive search consultants and the way they would like to be viewed by clients: as eminently well positioned to lead organizations and guide talented, ambitious executives to new heights.

Their backgrounds and working environs are about as disparate as possible, but Sherpa guides and executive search consultants share one significant characteristic: Both most often work behind the scenes, never garnering the credit they deserve. Much in the same way that wealthy individuals from around the world are celebrated for their mountaineering achievements with not much attention paid to their guides, most corporate press releases announcing the hiring of a new senior executive fail to mention—let alone credit—the executive search consultant who helped guide the hiring process and lent valuable external perspective to it.

The parallel between Sherpa mountain guides and executive search consultants rings true because of the complexity, difficulty, and seriousness of the challenge, and the way a single misstep can lead to downfall. The higher climbers go on Mount Everest, the more likely they are to die from oxygen deprivation, frostbite, exhaustion, or injury. So too, the higher up the corporate organizational chart recruiting takes place, the more consequential that executive search process becomes for employees, vendors, shareholders, and the executive who is ultimately hired.

Given the shifting competitive landscape brought about by continuing globalization, there are real parallels between the unknown or difficult terrain of the world's tallest mountain peaks—to cite a portion of one of the dictionary definitions of the word *Sherpa*—and the similarly unknown and difficult terrain of the shifting global market for executive talent.

FEARS OF LOSING LEADERSHIP TALENT

If the word *Sherpa* speaks accurately to the role executive search consultants play in elevating a company's senior talent, how then should I describe their role in pulling talented executives *out* of a company?

Because they rarely involve unemployed executives, the vast majority of search assignments that spell success for one corporate employer are considered a form of piracy by another, which saw one of its best-performing executives leave—perhaps to join a direct competitor.

One very public debate, described below, illustrated how the work and influence of executive recruiters impinges on important issues like executive compensation, corporate governance, shareholder rights, and executive privilege. It also brought to light corporate fears about how the disclosure of top non-executive salaries would enable executive recruiters and competing corporations to more easily recruit away top talent, potentially dealing major blows to corporate earnings and shareholder confidence in a company's management and stock.

The anything-goes executive pay environment that until recently pervaded corporate America was replete with multimillion-dollar severance deals and wink-and-nod approvals of the backdating of stock option grants. To tame this "wild west," the Securities and Exchange Commission (SEC) required increased disclosure of executive pay and perks, voting to force public companies to divulge the total annual pay for their CEO, CFO, and the next three highest-paid executives, effective December 15, 2006.

But the SEC bowed to unprecedented pressure in removing the so-called Couric Clause, named for CBS television anchor Katie Couric, who was then rumored to be on the verge of signing a five-year, $15 million deal with CBS. That provision of the ruling would have required a company to reveal the total pay given to as many as three non-executive employees whose compensation exceeded that of any of its top five executives. What was the chief argument against the Couric Clause? Big media companies like CBS, Viacom, and Disney told the SEC that the disclosure of such pay packages would make it easier for recruiters (in executive search consulting firms and rival corporations alike) to conduct talent raids or "liftouts" of entire teams of people based on their knowledge of top-earning employees' pay. The concern also voiced by Kellogg, the world's largest breakfast cereal maker, was that rival employers could figure out how much it would cost them to lure a corporate star of the same magnitude as Couric.

In a March 16, 2006, comment letter posted on the SEC Web site, Jim Markey, Kellogg's vice president and chief international and securities counsel, wrote: "Employee compensation information is very sensitive and the disclosure of the total compensation paid to a non-executive employee, such as a salesperson, could cause employee morale issues and provide our competitors with sensitive information that could be used to solicit the employment of our salespeople at the expense of Kellogg Company and its shareholders." And that's no stretch, as one noted academic opines that recruiting executives from outside "is a way of stealing intellectual capital from another company."

Companies like News Corp. and Dreamworks Animation also lent their significant political clout to the fight against the Couric Clause, warning that such a disclosure rule would inhibit sought-after executive candidates who wished to keep their financial affairs out of the public domain from joining public companies where they might indeed earn more than the top five corporate officers.

Had it gone into effect, the Couric Clause would have created a whole new information stream from which the researchers who work within the walls of nearly every executive search consulting firm could cherry-pick data with which to develop compelling enticements and thus clear the way for the recruitment of a top corporate executive.

THE SUPPLY AND DEMAND OF EXECUTIVE TALENT

The market for senior business executives is seriously inefficient, which is why corporate employers often fear executive search consultants and some even retain them simply and solely to prevent their luring away top talent. This market is driven mostly by forces external to the employer organization, and, as noted, it is rigged to favor the selection of people who already hold or who have held the same title in a similarly sized organization.

In the world of sports, talent and God-given physical attributes combine to sort the professionals from the amateurs from the weekend warriors. But in the worlds of twenty-first-century business, politics, and organizational life in general, talent isn't the only road to the top. Today's organizations are led by individuals of widely divergent talent sets and abilities, and most would not have risen to the top without some measure of at least one of the following: hard work, a mentor, political savvy, cultural savvy, financial backing, nepotism, good looks, a degree from an elite school, a good friend who works as an executive search consultant, and, yes, a certain degree of luck, or what some have called "being in the right place at the right time."

Any combination of those success factors might well qualify an upright executive for a new leadership challenge, but it is because those measures can't be recorded on a score sheet or easily compared to a rival's rise through the ranks that an increasing number of voices can be heard speaking out about executive compensation.

SEC chairman Christopher Cox, in remarks presented to the Council of Institutional Investors in March 2006, acknowledged the divide that separates entertainment and business professionals in the public discourse about appropriate pay for outstanding talent. "The truth is, we don't begrudge athletes and the Hollywood glitterati their outrageously high salaries," Cox said. He added, "In a market economy, supply and demand should, and normally do, dictate what people are paid. If an athlete's skills are exceptional even when measured in the context of global competition—and if the supply of similarly talented players is scarce—it stands to reason that individual will be highly compensated."[4]

That's certainly music to the ears of executive search consultants because it perpetuates the notion that organizations (and, by extension, their shareholders) have to pay through the nose to recruit and employ a top executive who might stay only two or three years, if that long. It also perpetuates the idea that talent at the executive level is scarce, a message that has all but guaranteed the succession of top leadership posts through a lineage of privileged people already granted some measure of corporate power, most likely by some other employer. And the only way to get them to agree to a trade is to pay top dollar.

The big difference, Cox went on to explain, citing the work of Lucian Bebchuk of Harvard and Jesse Fried of the University of California, Berkeley, is that unlike those who recruit agented sports figures or Hollywood stars, "boards of directors of public companies don't always negotiate at arm's length with their executives. And as a result, the executives are often able to influence the level of their own compensation."[5]

Beyond what executives are paid, says Peter M. Felix, CBE, a former CEO of the British-American Chamber of Commerce and president of the Association of Executive Search Consultants (AESC), the work of executive search consultants to facilitate executive mobility is a hallmark of the free market economy. "Most successful market economies have a number of key characteristics in common—free capital markets, dependable legal systems, a democratic political structure, open education and an unrestricted labor market which permits and encourages executive mobility," Felix says. "Executive mobility is crucial to a dynamic economy since it unleashes talent that might otherwise be constrained and promotes the cross-fertilization of ideas and creative thinking. Without continually seeking out executives with managerial skills and innovative ideas, an economy is prone to stagnation and restriction in its orientation and outlook."[6]

Executive mobility . . . unleashes talent that might otherwise be constrained and promotes the cross-fertilization of ideas and creative thinking.

Further to the influence of his association's member firms, he adds: "The free market economy must thrive on competition and the optimum use of available resources. Amongst those resources the one with the largest multiplier for success is the senior executive. . . . Today the executive search consultant is well placed [as a market intermediary] to oil the wheels between demand and supply and to act as honest broker to the parties involved."

MANDATE FOR CHANGE

There are other reasons why the business of executive recruiting needs a second look. Besides corporations' alternately loving and hating executive search consultants for the work they do, consider the findings of one recent search profession survey: Only 46 percent of the corporate leaders who had retained executive search consultants said they were fully satisfied with the outcome of their work.

Part of the blame should be shouldered by the executive search consulting community because its members have almost universally failed to demonstrate how either the tenure or the performance of an externally recruited executive compares to that of one promoted from within. Add to that the consultants' occasionally inconsistent performance, their failure to communicate the progress of search assignments to their clients, their inflated egos, and their general distaste for working with HR staff, and you begin to get a sense of why innovation, differentiation, and performance metrics that resonate with corporate employers are all key to the future of the executive search consulting profession. After all, it is a profession that lacks certification, licensure, government regulation, industry oversight, and even a single university degree program dedicated to its practice, but it nonetheless influences the future direction of corporations large and small.

But part of the blame must also be laid at the feet of the legions of corporate executives—including many CEOs and board nominating committees—who bring to the process of selecting and retaining search firms their own misperceptions, biases, and agendas. Managing client expectations has always been one of the biggest challenges for executive search consultants. In addition, until very recently, most corporate employers failed to support the integration of a new executive hire with a formal onboarding or performance feedback plan, and that hasn't helped the cause of orderly recruiting, either.

The problem is that six- or seven-figure executives, more than anyone else employed by a corporation, are expected to hit the ground running almost immediately upon their hiring, in part because of their credentials, experience, and past achievements, and in part because of what they're being paid. These lofty, often unrealistic expectations make the work of executive search consultants even more challenging and consequential.

Many times, the failure of an organization to properly support a new executive in the formative first months on the job leads to the scapegoating of the search consultant—who, despite having possibly orchestrated a world-class talent bake-off—may well have to wonder why the client hasn't called back. No one on the inside was willing to say "mea culpa," so all the trouble was piled on the conveniently absent consultant.

IN SEARCH OF BEST PRACTICES

The bottom line is that executive recruiters and the corporate leaders they serve need to reassess how they do business with one another and find consensus on what leadership really means to shareholders, employees, and customers. In this age of increased shareholder and regulatory scrutiny of boardroom and governance affairs, providing greater transparency into the management succession process will go a long way toward rebuilding the public trust, shareholder support, and employee morale that dissipated in the wake of corporate scandals.

Prior to almost any announcement by a big company that it has hired a new CEO, phone calls are made and contracts are signed with executive search firms to recruit the company's next leader or otherwise vet the external talent market against the credentials of a favored inside candidate. Little fanfare attends that process—unless management's choice of a successor to the CEO or some other powerful executive botches the job.

Who among the entire population of New Orleans paid much attention to the nomination of Michael Brown as director of the Federal Emergency Management Agency in January 2003? Brown made headlines when he was relieved of his command after the government's bungled response to Hurricane Katrina in August 2005 and ultimately resigned after questions surfaced about the truthfulness of his résumé and of statements in an online biography. A lot of New Orleans residents might have had something to say about Brown's appointment had they known more about his questionable qualifications for the job. It just wasn't apparent to them some two and a half years earlier that

Brown's job performance and qualifications for the United States's top emergency response job would so directly affect their lives. But it did.

Such is the seriousness of leadership succession issues. In government, leaders directly affect the health and safety of people and families. In corporations, they decide the future of shareholders, employees, vendors, and customers.

Anyone who has a job or relies on a spouse's job, who owns stock in a company, who sells goods or services to another company, or who simply has a passing interest in the question of whether more women and minorities will be given the chance to lead should take interest in the process that elevates individuals to positions of leadership in organizations that touch their lives. However, this is exactly the kind of issue most people choose not to trouble themselves with until they're told that they or their spouse will be reporting to a new executive the company has hired from the outside. Or until the stocks that populate their mutual funds are sunk by a scandal involving a CEO with an inflated or invented work history. Or until business, government, or some other policy starts to fly in the face of their common sense.

OVER THE HORIZON

The end of corporate management succession as we've known it will come at an eventful time for corporate HR professionals, who, much like executive search consultants, have been the subject of increasing calls to reassess and perhaps even reinvent the way they work.

One of the ways in which corporations around the world will improve and significantly alter their approaches to attracting, recruiting, developing, and promoting top executive talent will be to raise the bar for their internal recruiting practices up to the standard of quality delivered by the very best executive search consulting firms. But that won't be possible unless corporations elevate the mission, profile, and voice of the human capital function that most often takes up exclusive residence within the walls of the HR department.

Executive search consultants and senior management staffing and talent acquisition executives who work for the corporation should be strategic allies when it comes to meeting the organization's current and future leadership talent needs. But that partnership—which, to date, has largely failed to bridge the inherent divide between outside experts and well-qualified employees—won't have a chance to grow unless (1) HR is made a strategic partner in the company's future growth, and (2) search consultants develop the kinds of metrics that clearly demonstrate the return on corporate investment in their work and help HR make the case for continued investment in the people side of the business.

The strain on both executive search consultants' and HR professionals' relationships with top corporate leaders and line managers can be overcome if the external and internal parties to the corporate succession process work as partners rather than adversaries, which is often the case these days and is yet another dynamic that squeezes the chances for success with external hiring.

Much of the promise of this partnership stems from the need for corporations around the world to spend more of their time developing a plan to meet their future leadership needs, something that recent surveys suggest they've been avoiding at their peril. The business of management succession, as some have learned, is about much more than filling vacant executive-level jobs. In fact, it requires a more thoughtful, more inclusive, and far more forward-looking commitment by the corporation to assess its market position, its competitive strengths and weaknesses, its market dynamics, and its goals for the future than most employers have ever found time to engage in.

The threats and opportunities of the world business stage present themselves faster now than they ever have, so they're beginning to dictate that corporations make decisions faster, recruit faster and more effectively, and adjust to inevitable change more deftly than in the past.

International developments in social, political, and corporate circles now reverberate throughout the business markets. As a result, even the most trusted, seemingly best-performing global executives spend their nights worrying whether their workforce is properly aligned to the challenge and capable of mastering the skills it may need to rely on should the demands of customers, governments, and shareholders change the rules of the game—which they may at a moment's notice.

Filling the executive talent pipeline is now a critical competency for corporate recruiters and external search consultants. That's because, for many mature companies and markets, the only substantial growth potential lies in overseas markets—and the best source of management-level talent resides locally in those markets. It's also a matter of life and death. Death, that is, in the sense of our human mortality—and the fact that companies such as Gillette and McDonald's have already experienced the misfortune of seeing their top officers die suddenly. In the case of McDonald's, its board had planned for potential calamity and so was prepared when its sixty-year-old leader Jim Cantalupo succumbed suddenly to a heart attack in April 2004. A successor was named within hours of Cantalupo's untimely death.

The international stock markets and global investors cherish stability, which is why the transition of any senior executive is always watched closely, especially by financial analysts. So when the untimely death of a CEO seems to catch a corporation entirely off-guard, the company risks not only the ire of and a potential loss of faith among shareholders and analysts but a likely drop in its share price.

Given increasing calls for corporate social responsibility, management transitions will be eyed by far more stakeholders in the future than ever before. That increased scrutiny alone should usher in the end of corporate management succession as we've known it. It should also serve as a catalyst for new ways of recruiting and promoting "the best of the best" to meet the leadership challenges of tomorrow.

Business leaders are taking the reins of businesses across the world from their country of origin. Global business fluency, international work experience, cultural sensitivity, and language skills are in high demand, and American executives without those twenty-first-century superstar requisites will find themselves increasingly on the outside looking in when it comes to senior management succession.

Recruiting the leaders of tomorrow will force executive search consultants to search for the best-qualified leaders, whether they work and reside nearby or halfway around the world. The task will also demand that corporate employers open their minds to the kinds of human and professional experiences that talented outsiders can bring to help the organization achieve a solid and long-running human capital advantage.

The end of executive recruiting as we've known it will forever change corporate management succession and executive search consulting, which stands as arguably the single most important form of management consulting engaged by employer organizations today and one that will only grow in importance in years to come.

3

DISNEY'S EXECUTIVE DECISION

Their willingness to be led around by the nose would be amusing if there weren't so much at stake.

ROY E. DISNEY AND STANLEY P. GOLD[1]

The opening line of a joint public statement issued on July 8, 2005, by the Walt Disney Company, Roy E. Disney, and Stanley P. Gold was concise, cordial, and utterly resolute: "The Walt Disney Company, Roy E. Disney and Stanley P. Gold announced today that they have agreed to put aside the differences that have characterized their relationship over the past several years."

The statement closed a difficult chapter in the history of one of the world's most admired companies; one whose stock is held by millions of people around the world, whose creative innovations have inspired generations, and whose influence has in no small measure shaped the global media and entertainment industry. It summarily silenced a distraction that had been a public nuisance for Disney management for at least two years. It also quashed a looming courtroom battle that was set to unfold just a few weeks later.

CHARM OFFENSIVE

The July 8 announcement heralded the first decisive leadership achievement of Robert A. Iger, the Disney executive who had been selected four months earlier to succeed the company's outgoing CEO, Michael D. Eisner. Eisner had become a lightning rod for shareholder discontent and had been blamed for inciting an exodus of talented Disney employees.

In preparing to take the reins of Disney leadership from Eisner, CEO-in-waiting Iger went on a sensible and high-impact charm offensive aimed at soothing lingering tensions within the company. But it was Iger's diplomatic efforts to broker a truce with dissident shareholders-turned-plaintiffs Stanley Gold and Roy Disney (nephew of Walt Disney, who had cofounded the company in 1923) that ended the duo's shareholder lawsuit. That suit had challenged Eisner's role in the search to find his successor, called into question Iger's selection as the company's next chief executive, and, in an unprecedented fashion, threatened to expose the secret dealings of Disney's chosen executive search consultants and their role in deciding who was to lead the company.

Yet while the public statement that was delivered to the media and posted on SaveDisney.com, the dissident shareholders' Web site, saved the company millions in legal fees and spared it the damaging headlines that might have resulted from the trial, it failed to address key management-oriented concerns voiced by shareholders. It ignored issues that had been raised at the company's contentious 2004 annual meeting in Philadelphia, where 45 percent of voting shareholders essentially rendered a vote of no confidence in Eisner. It also answered few of the serious questions raised by Roy Disney and his financial adviser, Stanley Gold, in the months that followed—questions they then believed could only be answered under oath in a courtroom in Delaware, where the company is incorporated.

Questions like these: Did CEO Eisner manipulate the executive search that resulted in Disney's board's selection of Iger as his successor? Had members of the board made false statements to Disney shareholders about the CEO search in an effort to induce them to vote for the incumbent board at the 2004 annual meeting and to stop Roy Disney and Stanley Gold from putting up an alternate slate of directors at that meeting? What roles did the board's chairman and its search committee play in the search assignment? What might be revealed about the executive search process in the notes, files, presentation materials, and sworn testimony of the executive search consultants who were to have contacted, interviewed, and analyzed leading candidates—both inside and outside the existing Disney talent pool—for Disney's top job?

And, surely more tantalizing for Wall Street analysts, the business media, and the investing community, these additional questions: Who among the most-heralded CEOs of America's largest multinational corporations had taken the executive recruiters' calls? Who among them had expressed enough interest to warrant an interview with the Disney board's search committee, and why? And who, if any, among the external candidates was given fair and serious consideration? Or, as is sometimes the case, was the entire executive search process conducted as a false front or as a symbolic corporate ritual designed to placate angry shareholders and legitimize the promotion of an internal candidate?

It's entirely realistic to visualize an extremely narrow but nonetheless well-known set of potential contenders for the Disney CEO job and an even shorter short list of final candidates. That's because such a high-profile CEO search is almost always directed by the company's board—turning the process into more of a game of "fetch" than "search"—and largely limited to candidates with experience as CEO of an international company of similar size or larger.

The Walt Disney Company board announced in March 2005 that Iger was unanimously elected CEO and would take over upon Eisner's retirement. This was unsurprising, given that Iger had joined the company in 2000 as president, COO, and board member, and as a member of the company's executive management committee.

"After a lengthy, thorough and professional selection process, comparing both internal and external candidates against our criteria for

CEO, I am pleased to announce the decision of The Walt Disney Board of Directors to select Robert Iger as the company's next chief executive officer," George J. Mitchell, chairman of the board and a former U.S. senator from Maine, said in a March 13, 2005, company press release. Mitchell himself had been a target for dissident shareholders at the company's fractious 2004 annual meeting, as nearly 26 percent of shareholders withheld their votes for his incumbent seat on the Disney board. That 2004 meeting cost Eisner his chairman's seat, but it didn't stop the board from awarding Eisner a $7.2 million bonus the same year, nor did it prevent Mitchell's friends on the board from later appointing Mitchell as chairman of the board.

But Disney and Gold weren't buying it. They smelled a rat in the house of the world's best-known mouse. So, in addition to the company, they sued Iger, Eisner, and company directors Judith L. Estrin, John S. Chen, Alwyn B. Lewis, Monica C. Lozano, George J. Mitchell, and Fr. Leo J. Donovan, S.J., individually for fraud and breach of duty of disclosure in connection with the board's public statements about the search for a replacement for Eisner.

Disney and Gold wanted the court's intervention to void the 2005 board election and to compel the company to hold another election for directors after full and fair disclosure of all material facts about the CEO selection process. Disney and Gold also asked the Delaware Court of Chancery to enjoin the company and its board from changing either Eisner's or Iger's compensation or employment contracts.

In a ruling clearing the way for the lawsuit, the Honorable William B. Chandler III, chancellor of the Delaware Court of Chancery, established, according to a statement posted on Disney and Gold's SaveDisney.com Web site: "plaintiffs have alleged facts suggesting that the company's board did not go about the process of searching for a new CEO with 'open minds,' without prior determinations and giving 'full consideration' to external candidates. The complaint alleges that only one external candidate was interviewed, that Mitchell told [a] candidate 'she was not a serious candidate,' and that Eisner's presence at interviews of external candidates, 'was intended to chill and did chill full consideration of qualified external candidates for the position of CEO.'" Plaintiff Disney identified that candidate as none other than eBay president and CEO Meg Whitman, a media darling and one of the world's most respected CEOs—and one with the XX chromosome pattern to boot. *Fortune* would later report that Whitman's name was indeed near or at the top of Disney's chosen executive search firm's A-list.[2]

The judge's finding continued: "Should these allegations be proven, plaintiffs could be entitled to the relief they seek because the board's statements materially misled plaintiffs with respect to the board's intent to conduct a bona fide executive search process."

BONA FIDE EXECUTIVE SEARCH CONSULTING

The world's top executive recruiters—or executive search consultants, as they prefer to be known—make their living off the long-perpetuated failure of organizations everywhere to develop executive talent from within. And for a lot of reasons, whether for organizational or career purposes, you just can't get anywhere in the twenty-first-century business world without them. The Disney directors certainly knew that to be the case, and they understood that their interest in conducting a "thorough and professional selection process" required that executive search consultants be a major part of the game plan.

No matter what the economic environment, the best-performing companies (which are usually the best ones to work for, as well) are fueled by innovation, creativity, and brainpower. It's really all about talent. Talented individuals at the executive end of the organizational chart, and those who might eventually be recruited into it, create, control, or influence the company's resources and its strategic agenda. Along with those responsibilities comes the potential to transform the organization and help it drive positive results for shareholders, employees, vendors, and others.

Into the usually steady but sometimes inconsistent hands of the executive search consultant go the responsibilities of knowing the hiring organization as though from the inside, presenting its most important and most compelling executive job opportunities to highly qualified (and almost always gainfully employed) candidates, and then choreographing interviews and assessments that shape the decision of which candidates to recommend to the hiring organization.

Long a barometer of organizational climate and performance, the executive search consulting business is one that trades on access to senior executives and knowledge of turmoil and distress among their ranks. As one longtime practitioner puts it, "Search consultants are often the first to learn of corporate scandal because people flee companies and talk to recruiters."

Even under the best of circumstances, the average 120-day executive search assignment can put a strain on an organization. In the words of one executive search consultant, "Wall Street, the directors, and the remaining company executives are nervous until they know who is going to be steering the ship."[3] Whenever an organization hires or promotes an executive, people in various parts of the organization start wondering who their new boss will be, if they'll get along or clash, and whether they'll still have (or want) their job come Monday morning.

Search consultants are often the first to learn of corporate scandal because people flee companies and talk to recruiters.

MASTER INTERMEDIARIES

So why the need for executive search consultants? CEOs (and, increasingly, corporate legal departments) often prefer to keep the job of lifting executive talent from the competition in the hands of a capable recruiting professional who is off their corporate payroll. Keeping that sensitive but vital task at arm's length distances the raiding employer from the act, and may in fact prevent competitors from engaging in a direct, potentially bitter, and unseemly war for each other's top leaders and emerging executive talent.

The decision to promote from within or tap search firm databases is usually a matter of determining whether insider talent is up to the job. It may also be a question of whether significant structural, political, cultural, or symbolic change—better led by a currently unaffiliated outsider—is required.[4] Going outside also buffers the hiring organization from having to deal with the post-search concerns (or perhaps even sour grapes) of the dozens, often hundreds of individuals who are contacted as information sources, referrers, or candidates for a single executive job vacancy.

Using an intermediary also prevents the kind of embarrassment the CEO or the board might feel if top executive prospects repeatedly turn down the offer. In many respects, the executive search consultant serves as an effective filter on the market, requiring client companies to address only those executives who meet or exceed the desired profile outlined in the job specification ("spec") or mandate that is drawn up before the launch of any executive search assignment, and who express sufficient interest to make it worthwhile for both sides to talk.

But it's also a question of what executive search consultants bring to the table. They are specialized management consultants who are retained on an exclusive basis by hiring organizations intent on breaking the status quo, improving corporate performance, benchmarking internal candidates against the external talent market, or simply replacing an executive—that is, a business leader whose job pays at least $200,000 per year, and quite often much more. The executive recruiters' mission: locate a top-notch executive willing to step into a new position or into a vacancy created by resignation, retirement, death, illness, or dismissal.

At the highest level in organizations, executive search consultants facilitate the CEO search process like chess masters, orchestrating the timing of every move and anticipating a variety of outcomes. Outside the CEO position, however, theirs is a much more complicated matchmaking process of searching the globe to find the right executive at the right time for the right opportunity with the right company. Executive search consultants control access to a large number of the world's highest-paying and most coveted jobs. Simply put, their judgments help make some careers blockbusters and block the development of others.

The use of a consultant is best reserved for those situations when an executive-level job can't be filled by the promotion of a current employee. All too often, however, businesses engage consultants as a first option. Tens of thousands of organizations worldwide turn to executive search consultants every year to substantiate, coordinate, and support the hiring of external executive candidates. Others engage consultants to benchmark the quality of internal executive talent and affirm and legitimize a promotion from within—like the one that put Bob Iger in charge of the Walt Disney Company.

Executive search consultants' . . . judgments help make some careers blockbusters and block the development of others.

"THE MICE ON DISNEY'S BOARD"

Roy Disney and Stanley Gold shouldered the concerns of many disgruntled Disney shareholders after the two resigned from the company's board (on November 30 and December 1, 2003, respectively). Roy Disney and his family, court records indicated, held Disney company stock that in May 2005 was worth more than $750 million. Roy Disney believed those combined holdings made him the single largest shareholder, or at least one of the largest shareholders, in the company.

One can easily understand why Roy Disney would monitor the company's financial performance and its rate of return to shareholders. One can also imagine the sinking feeling he must have experienced when Disney's top leadership presided over a serious loss in the value of his Disney holdings, as the company had started to underperform in 1996. As his May 2005 court complaint detailed: "The decline of the Company's performance under the Eisner/Iger stewardship is set forth in the Company's 2005 proxy statement, which discloses that a $148 investment in the Company in fiscal year 2000, when Mr. Iger was appointed President and COO, would have been worth only $91 by the end of the 2004 fiscal year."

Besides blaming Eisner, however, Roy Disney and Stanley Gold might also have blamed themselves. After all, they had played no small roles in luring Eisner to Disney in 1984, and together had ranked among Eisner's most vocal supporters. Now Disney and Gold wanted Eisner gone.

Six months after the 2004 shareholder uprising they spearheaded, Roy Disney and Stanley Gold got their wish. Or so it appeared when Eisner announced on September 9, 2004, his plan to retire from his CEO role. The next day, under a headline that read "Eisner Gives Disney His Notice," CBS News reported: "Eisner has strongly endorsed Disney President Robert Iger as a potential successor. But the board could look to other executives in the company or even former Disney executives who now lead their own companies. Likely candidates include Paul Pressler, CEO of Gap. Inc., or Meg Whitman, CEO of eBay Inc. Former Viacom President Mel Karmazin and News Corp. chief operating officer Peter Chernin are also often mentioned as possible successors."[5]

Four days after Eisner's announcement, Roy Disney and Gold sent a letter to the nonemployee members of the Disney board, encouraging them "to engage in an independent worldwide search for a new CEO and complete it before the 2005 Annual Stockholders Meeting." Their letter also stated that they intended to propose an alternate slate of directors at that meeting if the board failed to "immediately engage an independent executive recruiting firm to conduct a worldwide search for a talented CEO and concurrently announce that Michael Eisner will leave the Company at the conclusion of that search."

The duo's repeated use of the word *independent* in describing the ideal firm to conduct a global executive search was interesting because it was uninformed. Executive search consultants are paid by hiring organizations, and, ultimately, they answer to the CEO. Apparently, both Roy Disney and Stanley Gold believed the executive recruiters who would coordinate the Disney CEO search would be equally answerable to vocal dissident shareholders trying to dislodge a sitting CEO as they would be to the insiders who controlled the purse strings and who would be most responsible for seeing that their invoices were paid on time.

Yet the pressure they exerted on the Disney board seemed to work. On September 21, 2004, the company announced:

> *The Board will engage in a thorough, careful, and reasoned process to select as the next CEO the best person for the company, its shareholders, employees, customers, and for the many millions of others who care so much about The Walt Disney Company. To achieve its objective, the Board will: 1) Engage an executive search firm to assist it in selecting a CEO who possesses the qualities and experience the Board believes are necessary for this important position [and], 2) Consider both internal and external candidates. Bob Iger is the one internal candidate. He is an outstanding executive and the Board regards him as highly qualified for the position. However, the Board believes that the process should include full consideration of external candidates as well. . . . The Board regards its responsibility on succession as so significant that all members should participate actively and fully in the entire process; and each has committed to do so.*

Further, according to court documents, Roy Disney and Stanley Gold took the Disney board "at its word" that it would oversee a bona fide search process, and they shelved plans to campaign for a full rival slate of nonincumbent directors at the company's 2005 annual meeting. But shortly after that meeting, Roy Disney and Stanley Gold claimed, they "heard from a reliable source that external CEO candidates would be interviewed in the presence of Eisner." On March 10, 2005, they wrote to the Disney board to express concerns about this possibility. Three days later, the company announced that Iger would succeed Eisner as CEO, and that Eisner would move up the date of his previously planned retirement date by one year, to September 30, 2005.

Roy Disney and Stanley Gold didn't waste any time preparing their response: an op-ed piece titled "The Mice on Disney's Board" in the March 17, 2005, editions of the *Los Angeles Times.* They wrote, "Disney directors promised shareholders 'a thorough, careful and reasoned process to select as the next CEO the best person for the company'"—a process, they added, that "should include full consideration of external candidates." And when doubts were raised about how objective and inclusive the search really was, board chairman Mitchell piously insisted that he and his fellow directors were conducting it "in good faith, with open minds and without any prior determination or preconditions."

The diatribe continued:

> *Of course, we've since learned that the search involved only one real candidate—Eisner's handpicked heir apparent, Disney President Robert Iger. By caving in to Eisner's demand that he be allowed to sit in on interviews of potential successors, by not even attempting to interview a single outside candidate until after its annual meeting in February, by refusing to insist that Eisner commit to leaving the company as soon as the new CEO was named, and by not objecting to the aggressive public relations campaign Eisner had his minions wage on Iger's behalf, the board effectively endorsed the notion that "the fix was in" and virtually guaranteed that no serious outside executive would be willing to be considered for the job.*

Roy Disney and Stanley Gold raised the stakes for Disney and its shareholders when they sued the company and certain members of its board of directors on May 9, 2005. The executive search consultants who were hired to coordinate that search now faced the prospect of having the private details of their work for Disney—and by extension, their profession—exposed to the light of day and the peering eyes of jurors for the first time ever. The legal battle was set to begin in August 2005.

"BECAUSE OF MY EYE"

Given its tremendous influence over the selection of institutional leaders around the world, the business of executive search consulting truly is everyone's business. But it has always been a clandestine, cloak-and-dagger pursuit because of the important, sensitive, and extremely confidential nature of its clients' revelations.

Knowing how to keep a secret is a hallmark of the executive search consultant's business, as is discreetly orchestrating methodical courtships between talented executives and their next potential employers. That's because few if any multinational corporations would publicly admit that they have a leadership deficit. And few high-flying executives would publicly admit that they would consider a new opportunity. There's simply too much at stake for both the hiring organization and the candidate.

The looming trial threatened to damage Disney's brand, demoralize its workforce, and drag down its stock price, and it also posed serious issues for the firm engaged to conduct the CEO search. The Disney legal battle would not only force its executive search consultants to reveal their full involvement in the CEO search but also prompt the potential outing of any executives who might have interviewed for the position, thereby jeopardizing their existing job. The Disney case also forewarned of a new legal precedent that might make executives being courted for top jobs with other companies around the world uneasy about talking with executive search consultants, lest they be identified in a distant courtroom.

The prospect of the revelation of an executive search consultant's secret dealings with clients on so public a stage and involving so well-known an institution as the Walt Disney Company would be historic for a professional service business that has by and large successfully managed its affairs—and the supersensitive affairs of its clientele—under the radar screen.

Even now, few companies mention the executive search consulting firm that helped make a newly announced hire happen, although that number is growing. Despite the fact that the shares of publicly owned executive search firms are traded on the New York Stock Exchange, the NASDAQ, and the Canadian stock exchanges, few people outside the executive search business and the executive ranks of the world business community regularly pay much attention. When that does happen, it's increasingly the result of a magazine or newspaper article profiling an accomplished executive search consultant or extolling the six-figure, jet-set lifestyle that tends to come with—and often enables—the job.

The business of executive search consulting first took root inside the walls of management consulting firms like McKinsey & Company and Booz Allen Hamilton in the years following World War I. It has long ignited the passions of entrepreneurs who left behind careers with the then Big 8 accounting firms and corporate personnel departments. Most of those big consulting and accounting juggernauts eventually jettisoned their executive search consulting businesses because they were simply a distraction, or because the fees they generated weren't enough to justify any recruitment-oriented entanglements with their lucrative consulting, accounting, and audit clients.

Today, more than forty thousand individuals work as partner- or consultant-level executive recruiters with roughly 9,500 executive search firms in 2,255 cities in eighty countries around the world.[6] The United States is home to the oldest, largest, and most highly fragmented market for executive recruiters' services, originating search fees that account for half of the $10 billion global executive search consulting market, and it is also by far the largest national exporter of executive jobs around the world.

Just twenty years ago, the largest global executive search firms were earning (or approaching) $50 million in professional fee revenue each year. Today, the same handful of global firms are eyeing more than $500 million in annual revenue each, and the profession is just one prolonged revenue surge or merger away from its first billion-dollar firm.

So how do executive recruiters see themselves? And what qualifies them to pass judgment on the quality and promise of the world's outstanding executive talent? For starters, most executive recruiters believe that their skill at people reading gets sharper with each client and candidate interaction, as does their confidence in the transferability of their candidates' skills, experience, and leadership qualities. After all, during the course of a career, an executive recruiter will interview thousands of potential job candidates in person, and perhaps a few thousand client-side executives from organizations near and far.

Their work conjures a story about a young couple, tourists on a leisurely drive between Madrid and Barcelona. They marvel not only at the beauty of the Spanish countryside, but also at the bounty of the seemingly innumerable, unattended melon fields that, during this particular time of year, line both sides of the road for as far as the eye can see. The couple eventually happens upon an elderly merchant selling melons by the side of the road. They stop and ask the man why, when they could casually take any melon along the route of their journey for free and entirely unnoticed, they should pay for one of his. To which the old man replies, "Because of my eye."

The same ability to spot the needle in a haystack, to discriminate a world-class executive from the rest, is one claimed almost without exception by executive search consultants. Instead of picking melons, these executive recruiters pick people, and in so doing, they cultivate careers and help organizations grow.

It is very serious work, and work that can be incredibly consequential. One of the early leaders of the executive search consulting profession put it this way: "Most resources are available to all companies. The great variable is the quality of management—it determines why some companies fail and others succeed."[7]

The best executive recruiters are change agents who help businesses organize and reorganize around executive talent, with an eye toward breaking up the status quo and improving the quality of management and the quality of results for shareholders. Hiring organizations pay them handsomely, as executive search consultants' fees are based on the salary and bonus earnings of the candidates they recruit.

A sampling of executive recruiters' promotional literature and Web sites captures much of the spirit of their hard work to connect the right executive with a compelling opportunity with the best employer at just the right time:

- "Our mission is to contribute to our clients' success by identifying men and women of uncommon ability and potential . . . individuals to whom our clients might not otherwise have access."[8]
- "Our clients entrust us with some of their most important, sensitive, and confidential management issues. We repay this trust by putting their interests above all else."[9]
- "When you entrust a firm to secure your company's most valuable resource, you need to know that the process is being managed by professionals who have the necessary experience and business acumen . . . we understand that management selection is key to achieving your business strategy."[10]

These days, the engagement of an executive search firm usually follows very closely the announcement of a CEO's resignation, death, or pending retirement (as in the case of the Walt Disney Company), and often the naming of an interim leader who'll oversee day-to-day operations until a permanent successor is promoted from within or recruited from the outside. Especially to jittery shareholders, the engagement of an executive search firm is reassuring news.

Harvard University's Rakesh Khurana notes: "The use of executive search firms signals to external stakeholders, such as stockholders, that a thorough and exhaustive process was employed in selecting the CEO. As one director put it, 'These days, when institutional investors are monitoring your every move, it is very important that the process appear to be a fair process and not a political process.' This pressure to demonstrate a fair process is so prevalent that executive search firms are often employed even when a known insider is the best candidate for the successor CEO."[11]

Our clients entrust us with some of their most important, sensitive, and confidential management issues.

A BROKERED TRUCE

The lawyers representing the Walt Disney Company, its executive search consultants, and plaintiffs Roy Disney and Stanley Gold all geared up for what looked in early July of 2005 to be an incredibly revealing and potentially embarrassing courtroom battle.

The executive recruiters were to be subpoenaed as part of the pretrial discovery process, and they were well aware that their depositions regarding their role in the Disney CEO search would expose their private records—most especially, their personal notes disclosing candidate names—to the searing light of the court and assembled media.

The prospect of that unprecedented outing of the finalist candidates for Disney's top job—who would have presented themselves as such to the company's search committee—was nothing short of explosive, as it threatened the existing livelihood of any participating leaders of other companies not chosen for the Disney post. And for the first time, it posed for the executive search business the threat of public disclosure of records its members have long considered (rightly or wrongly) akin to those protected by lawyer–client confidentiality. It had to be a nervous time for those involved on all sides of the looming trial . . . with the possible exception of CEO-in-waiting Robert Iger.

The employees and shareholders of the Walt Disney Company were introduced to Iger's leadership craft in the form of the truce he brokered through meetings with Roy Disney and Stanley Gold in the summer of 2005, which resulted in the dismissal of their lawsuit and the release of the July 8 joint public statement about the out-of-court settlement.

A statement issued on the dissidents' SaveDisney.com Web site noted that the two sides "agreed to put aside the differences that have characterized their relationship over the past several years." The statement indicated that in "reestablishing ties with him and his family, the company has named Roy E. Disney Director Emeritus and a consultant." The company also reaffirmed its intention to rotate committee members and chairpersons on its board committees, as required by its corporate governance guidelines.

As part of the deal, Disney and Gold agreed not to run a rival slate of directors nor submit shareholder resolutions for the next five years. The joint statement also indicated that the two men "agreed to dismiss all of their pending lawsuits against the Company." The statement continued: "In putting aside their differences, the Company noted Mr. Disney's longtime devotion to the Company and welcomed the reestablishment of a relationship with him and his family." It went on to announce that Disney and Gold had "expressed confidence in Mr. Iger's leadership, and as Mr. Eisner retires after 21 years with the company, they acknowledged his contribution to the company over the years."

QUESTIONS LEFT UNANSWERED

The joint public statement issued by the company and the former dissidents on July 8, 2005, silenced what had become a bitter dispute, and it served as a testament to Iger's leadership. But it also left many questions unanswered—questions that might have been raised by disillusioned Disney shareholders, and questions that might also have been raised about the way companies do business and how they conduct the very important business of executive management succession.

Questions like this: Why did Disney board chairman George Mitchell, who in September 2004 announced the board's plans for a "thorough, careful, and reasoned [selection] process," prevent—as has been reported by *Fortune*—its chosen search consultants from contacting external CEO candidates until four months into the search? And why had the board (with Eisner present, as Roy Disney described in his newspaper editorial and in his court complaint as having been "widely reported" by the media) interviewed only one external CEO candidate (Meg Whitman) during the search process?

Beyond the affairs of Disney, about which shareholders, the public, and the media have learned much only because of the tussle with dissident shareholders, the case raised questions about the state of corporate governance and the role of executive search consultants: Who should be given the opportunity to lead and why? What, if anything, can activist shareholders do to take back a company when they've lost confidence in the chief executive? What roles *do* the outgoing CEO, the board of directors, and the company's chosen executive search consultants play in the selection of an organization's new leader? What role, if any, *should* the departing CEO play? And how can a successful company and its executive management regain the trust of shareholders?

The answers to those questions—all central to the way big business does business in the global economy of the twenty-first century—carry with them implications that touch a wide range of issues. These include issues not yet addressed by international corporate governance reforms, such as the full range of shareholder rights as they relate to the complete, truthful, and timely disclosure of executive pay; corporate crisis management; investor relations; succession planning; and related issues about defining corporate leadership needs, the work of executive search consultants, and the extent to which a company like Disney influences the management practices of other global companies. These are all questions likely to have yielded unprecedented public disclosures about management succession, executive pay, and shareholder activism had the Disney case gone to trial.

The settlement of the Walt Disney Company's clash with Roy E. Disney and Stanley P. Gold was good news for the company, its employees, its shareholders, and its brand. It was also good news for the executive search consultants who had been retained by the company because it meant they wouldn't have to tell all in a Delaware courtroom. They could carry on their covert work to marry executive opportunity with leadership talent unabated and avoid what surely would have been an unprecedented and especially revealing courtroom drama.

4

THE HEADHUNTERS' IDENTITY CRISIS

There goes the greatest headhunter who ever lived.

ADMIRERS OF AN EXECUTIVE SEARCH CONSULTING PIONEER

The $10 billion global business of executive search consulting is the most influential form of management consultancy retained by organizations and business leaders worldwide—and it is also the most misunderstood. The truth is that executive search consultants have a serious image problem, and many of them don't even know it.

AN ESTABLISHED PROFESSION

Consultancy in executive leadership recruiting relies on significant business experience, market research, and personal and professional networks. These resources, it's worth repeating, put executive recruiters in an incredibly influential position from which to drive and direct—and to disrupt—the global search for leadership advantage.

The executive search consulting profession counts among its members more than its share of Ivy League alumni and graduates of the most heralded international business schools. Other clubby, predominantly middle-aged business professionals—accomplished business leaders, former management consultants, and corporate line executives—also populate it. But the field also includes many self-made men and women engaged in the pursuit of exceptional leadership opportunity.

The profession's alumni include a former member of the British Parliament, a former U.S. ambassador to Algeria, the personnel director for U.S. President Ronald Reagan (who brought executive search to the White House), a liberator of the Nazi concentration camp at Nordhausen, Germany, and a former CEO of the British-American Chamber of Commerce. Other former executive search consultants head the Asian Pacific American Institute for Congressional Studies and the Economic Strategy Institute, a Washington, D.C.–based public policy research organization studying the impact of globalization on international trade. Search consultants' collective influence radiates in all directions, touching nearly every corner of organizational leadership.

People currently engaged in executive search consulting include a relative of Antarctic explorer Ernest Shackleton, the father of internationally acclaimed recording artist Josh Groban, a former *Newsweek* publisher, the son of one of the U.S. Navy's most decorated admirals and the grandson of another, and a college fraternity brother of President George W. Bush. Executive search consultants have sat on the boards of Sony Corporation, the Chicago Salvation Army, Boston's Joslin Diabetes Center, several publicly traded energy companies, and numerous other for-profit and not-for-profit organizations. The ranks of executive recruiters also include former business executives and HR professionals who yearned for a measure of independence, an opportunity to see the world, and a dramatically higher personal income.

The opportunity for leadership recruiters was borne out by a Towers Perrin/*Corporate Boardmember* magazine survey report indicating that 35.5 percent of board directors were willing to pay "whatever it takes" to recruit a new CEO. And the search for outstanding people in a variety of functions is worth the cost, according to Alan Eustace, a vice president of engineering at Google, who told the *Wall Street Journal* that one top-notch engineer is worth "300 times or more than the average," since some of the company's best offerings—including Gmail and Google News—were started by a single person.[1]

Executive search consultants orchestrated the recruitment of Eric Schmidt as CEO of Google in 2001. The recruiters involved in that search assignment reaped a financial windfall worth nearly $130 million when Google went public in 2004 and they were allowed to cash in the stock warrants they had received as payment. And shareholders were rewarded when Google's stock topped $500 per share. Schmidt's holdings in the company have since been counted in the billions of dollars.

The effort executive search consultants put into choreographing leadership transitions, the way they (most often) help companies avoid poor recruiting decisions, and the riches they steer to world-class executives (and themselves) may provide some insight into why executive search consultants bring so much swagger to their work. After all, they've recruited some of the world's most powerful business leaders, so they have the confidence that they'll do it again—and perhaps a bit of overconfidence that they'll do it well into the future.

A PARADOXICAL PATH

But the executive search consulting business is also filled with paradoxes. For instance, while many executive search consultants boast degrees from the world's leading business schools (some executive search profession events could double as Harvard and Yale alumni reunions) and some belittle job candidates from "no-name schools," some of the highest-profile executive recruiters of all time—the champions of CEO recruiting, the rarified domain that often defines the profession—graduated from institutions such as the University of Scranton, Bradley University, Worcester Polytechnic Institute, Lafayette College, and Monmouth College.

Another paradox is that those who rank among the world's most image-conscious businesspeople can also, collectively, count themselves among the most image-challenged. Executive recruiters are both highly regarded and widely disparaged, for reasons both deserved and undeserved.

It might astound all but the cobbler's children that many of the practitioners of an enterprise so intensely focused on the management succession issues faced by organizations the world over find themselves wholly unprepared to hand over the reins of their own search firms to a new generation of leaders. They have—but may not recognize—an incredible opportunity to diversify the leadership recruiting business.

And, given their deft, delicate, and compassionate handling of the executive-level job candidates in whom their clients show the most interest, it is also a paradox that they so callously mishandle and even abandon so many of those who entertain their overtures regarding potential career opportunities but are not ultimately selected. And that's only scratching the surface of a decidedly untidy area for executive recruiters, most of whom completely ignore the petitioners who e-mail their résumés unsolicited.

FORGING A COLLECTIVE IDENTITY

Collectively, executive search consultants are a group of specialized management consultants charged with understanding both the market for executive talent and the cultural identity of their client hiring organizations. Their task is to broadcast the siren song of career and leadership opportunity to their own handpicked list of proven business executives with heavy organizational responsibilities, the vast majority of whom aren't looking for a new job. Some of these executives would rather be left unfound, being just the kind of people once described in an Intercontinental Hotels in-room television advertisement (referring to its many global business guests) as "successful people quietly shaping the world."

Executive search consultants are paid by one party to the management recruiting process but, ideally, if they do their job well, end up respected by both sides. They help their client companies hire the right executives at the right time at a fair price for their experience, character, intelligence, vision, and overall leadership ability. And, from one well-known CEO's perspective, their ability to close the deal is key because "the company [the executive is] leaving almost always is going to counter."

Says one corporate CEO of the senior management recruiting challenge: "We're looking for gazelles, not elephants." One longtime European search consultant says: "If we get the right people in the right job, we've won the game." And another recruiter contends that he creates "lasting win-win scenarios" for executives and the companies who hire them.

Executive recruiters are self-appointed but well-credentialed students of people and organizations who are responsible for interviewing, psychoanalyzing, and otherwise reading executive-level job candidates so as to peer into their souls and decide which of them should be introduced to which employer organizations. They are social butterflies and indefatigable road warriors on a mission to expose talented executives to compelling career opportunities and to build their clients' shareholder value by increasing the investment return of their leadership assets. The core of their work lies in discriminating how and why an organization's products or services, its intellectual and human capital, and its employment culture differ from those of all other organizations, and thoroughly researching why a handful of talented executives with just the right mix of credentials, experience, and ambition should be given the opportunity to lead or help lead that organization.

Yet executive search consultants have failed to fully comprehend how their collective identity has, over many years, been established and differentiated mostly by the confused perceptions of—and their more than occasional distasteful encounters with—countless corporations, boards of directors, HR executives, job candidates, media representatives, and others. Their continuing quest for credibility and broad recognition as members of an honorable profession remains a task not unlike some North American ice hockey leagues' uphill (and perhaps grudging) battles to convince prospective television viewers that their game is something other than a well-organized, partly fan-incited brawl featuring grown men on ice skates.

The term *search firm* has long described executive recruiting organizations. But today, the business media increasingly use that term to describe the work of Internet search engines like Google and Yahoo. Consider, for example, this news headline: "Yahoo to buy Chinese search firm."[2]

The individuals recruited by executive search consultants are also labeled or mislabeled, depending on whether they live up to the expectations of the hiring organization. The most highly regarded among them are often referred to using words such as *superstar, savior, miracle worker,* and *A player,* and others are sold as *change agents, turnaround specialists,* and *visionaries.* Those who fail miserably are often labeled simply a bad fit with the organization they joined.

THE TROUBLE WITH HEADHUNTERS

High on the list of identity problems for executive search consultants is that they are saddled with the term *headhunters,* an outdated but nonetheless widely used pejorative that conjures violent images of remote, warlike tribal groups (like something out of *National Geographic* or the Discovery Channel) or of baseball melees prompted by pitchers' deliberate throwing at batters' heads. The term does not suggest the civilized work of extraordinarily polished market-facing recruitment advisers to corporate management.

That moniker does greater damage to their group identity and does more to diminish their usually impeccable individual credentials than most executive search consultants have ever realized. Over the course of the executive search profession's history, practitioners have been tagged with grandiose labels—corporate "kingmaker" and "career maker"—as well as some rather unseemly ones. For example, the late professional services publisher Jim Kennedy (self-appointed watchdog of the executive recruiting field), who gave me my first glimpse of the profession, included "pirate" and "body-snatcher" in his *Lexicon of Executive Recruiting.*[3] None of those labels, however, has matched the durability and marginalizing staying power of the word *headhunter*, which today still points far more businesspeople to the search craft's practitioners than any other descriptor.

The global economy drives on slick branding, and language often serves to advance company, product, and service names that roll easily off the tongue. So it's easy to understand how "headhunter" could become part of the business vernacular and fodder for media headlines like "Clash of the Corporate Kingmakers" and "In the Headhunters' Sights."[4] It certainly fits a line of type more readily than the polysyllabic "executive search consultant" or "executive recruiter."

None of those labels has matched the durability and marginalizing staying power of the word *headhunter.*

Besides the media's penchant for the pejorative, corporate training sessions prod in-house corporate recruiters to "act like headhunters" when they try to find talent for their employers. One United Kingdom–based publisher distributes a newsletter titled *The Headhunter,* in which the use of that pejorative is extremely widespread and seemingly hard to replace.

Such is also the case in France and French-speaking countries around the world, where *chasseurs de têtes* ("hunters of heads") is the term used among business executives, journalists, and job candidates, while executive search consultants opt for the more accurate, descriptive, yet unwieldy *conseils en recrutement de cadres dirigeants par approche directe* ("counselors in the recruitment of top executives by direct approach").

One long-retired pioneer of the executive search consulting business believes that identity problems still haunt his former colleagues, but he acknowledges that those issues persist in large part because of the very nature of the business. "You're predatory when you're in the executive search business and somebody is going to think they got hurt," he says. His own feelings and sense of identity are stung by the praise uttered by well-intentioned fellow country club members who turn to friends and guests as he passes to say: "There goes the greatest headhunter who ever lived."

No matter the lengths to which some of the pioneers of the business went to explain that the practice of executive search consulting grew out of the much larger management consulting profession, or that it served leaders at the top of the organization chart, or that it was nearly always executed by individuals with impeccable credentials and experience, not everyone has received or necessarily agreed with the message. "It hasn't attracted universal admiration," says a longtime London search consultant, "but it has come a long way from its beginnings." Adds another recruiter, perhaps the problem is the way the business of executive recruiting forces one "to go out and disrupt people's lives."

A GROWING RESPECT

Retired search consultant Bill Gould worked for one of the world's largest search firms before launching his own boutique firm in New York City. A Harvard Business School alum who once received a lifetime achievement award from his executive recruiting peers, Gould recalls being involved in an association survey in the early 1970s. "At that time," he recalls, "people didn't want to say they had to work with headhunters."

Gould says the survey revealed just how hard executive search consultants would have to work to move the needle on perceptions about their credibility, professionalism, and effectiveness. "We came in below public relations, at the very bottom of the pile, in perceptions of service providers, with consulting firms like McKinsey and Booz Allen Hamilton at the top," recalls Gould. He believes the origin of the business term *headhunter* was a 1960s-era *Fortune* article that referred to executive recruiters' hunting of heads.

But the inclusion of an executive search practice within such a highly regarded firm as Booz Allen Hamilton presented some interesting internal challenges. It also presented some indication of the traction that search consultants were gaining with corporate clients and candidates alike.

Barbara Provus, whose twenty-five-year career in executive search consulting started in the executive recruiting practice of Booz Allen Hamilton, recalls being briefed on the results of a survey conducted for the firm in the late 1970s. The survey asked influential business leaders what came to mind about Booz Allen Hamilton when they heard or thought of its name. "The overwhelming response was 'executive search' . . . even though the search practice was clearly one of the smallest," Provus recalls. "The search practice touched more people than any other practice, perhaps up to two hundred people on every search assignment. We were pressing more flesh than any other part of the business."

Provus says her tenure with the company ended in 1980 when Booz Allen Hamilton sold off its executive search practice. The reality, she says, was that although the influence of the practice had grown to the point of shaping the firm's brand identity, it remained a tiny portion of the overall business. It also had the potential for conflict with the firm's major organization consulting studies (which sometimes pointed to personnel gaps) and questions about whether executives employed by the firm's consulting clients were off-limits to the firm's executive search consultants.

The search practice touched more people than any other. . . . We were pressing more flesh than any other part of the business.

A major breakthrough for the profession's reputation, Gould contends, came years later, when search consultants were retained by boards of directors to conduct CEO and director search assignments for some of the world's largest companies. "Directors started to trust search firms with their plans for the future," he says. And, over time, Gould says, executive search consulting "became more and more acceptable to the business world. Today, if you did that same perceptions survey, search would be right up there with the top consulting firms."

William H. "Mo" Marumoto, who over a thirty-year career in leadership recruiting became known as the dean of search consultants in Washington, D.C., paints an especially positive portrait of how executive recruiters are now recognized and relied on. "Corporations, associations, government, and nonprofits generally hold really high regard for search consultants," he says. "Generally speaking, I'd say the search business has really grown in stature over the years, and most of [those organizations] go to search whenever there's a big opening" in their management leadership. Marumoto says search consultants have made a significant impact on organizations, much like their cousins in management consulting, and that's evident in that "smart management always retains these two groups."

For a business that deals in the exclusive representation of client organizations, partnership with organizational leadership, and access to executive talent the world over, executive search consultants worldwide should hope for no less than to have anyone with whom they interact appreciate the sophistication, differentiation, and influence of their hard work.

AN ONGOING IDENTITY CRISIS

But that could be a hard sell for some. Many of the world's leading executive search firms rightly describe themselves as management consultants, and they work on behalf of corporate boards, chief executives, and other senior business leaders. Nonetheless, the principal cities of nearly every industrialized nation have executive recruiting firms that incorporate the word *headhunters* into their name.

Add to that the number of executive search consultants who refer to themselves as headhunters in conversation with corporate executives and executive-level job candidates and the fact that online searches on "headhunter" and its variants yield far more executive search leads than any other search term, and the conundrum presented by this matter of identity becomes clear. Says one luminary of executive search consulting: "I think ['headhunter' is] demeaning. I don't acknowledge it. But it's widely used. It isn't discouraged enough by the people who are in the business."

Danish executive search consultant Oluf C. Jacobsen, in publishing the first Scandinavian book on the business of executive search consulting in 1985, chose for its title *Headhunting: Executive Search.*[5] His firm, J-B International A-S, carried the words "Management Consultants" on its letterhead and brochures but nonetheless advanced the pejorative when it commissioned the acclaimed Danish graphic artist Per Arnoldi that year for a signature design promoting the profession. The result was a 20" by 28" poster of a large, bright red apple pierced by a yellow arrow, drawing parallels between the precision demonstrated by William Tell in shooting an arrow through the apple atop his son's head and that required of executive search consultants who must delicately approach top-performing, gainfully employed executives to present potential career opportunities. Across the top of the poster read one word: *Headhunting.*

AS OTHERS SEE THEM

Living, breathing executive search consultants aren't the only ones lending to the confusion. Motion pictures have yet to cast a headhunter as anything but the villain. In *Pursued* (2004), for example, Christian Slater plays a headhunter with a killer instinct. An online plot outline says: "A fast-rising hi-tech executive must protect his career and family from the ruthless tactics of a homicidal corporate headhunter."[6]

The husband-and-wife writing team of Ron and Janet Benrey have likewise chronicled the adventures and misadventures of their own contrivance, Philippa ("Pippa") Hunnechurch. The fictional protagonist runs Philippa Hunnechurch & Associates and makes a living "recruiting top-notch candidates for hard-to-fill corporate positions."[7] She identifies herself as a headhunter but gives seminars with titles like "How to Work Successfully with an Executive Recruiter," perhaps in a bid to draw more self-respecting executives who don't necessarily want their heads hunted.

The identity crisis that has long dogged executive search consultants and gradually morphed into an image problem has at least part of its genesis in the environment that executive search consultants have created for themselves. Perhaps in part to make up for their lack of professional certification, but largely to communicate a measure of prestige to hiring organizations and distinguished candidates, executive search consultants have invested heavily in the accoutrements of material success. For some, it's a matter of demonstrating that their firm is a standout in a cottage profession that has virtually no barriers to entry. Their sometimes narcissistic and oftentimes trend-setting efforts to impress with posh offices, tailored suits, and exclusive club memberships rank executive search consultants among some of the world's most image-conscious business professionals. Just ask anyone who has ever known, partnered with, or been recruited by one.

When John A. Byrne of *BusinessWeek* wrote his 1986 book on the corporate management search business, it went to print as *The Headhunters.*[8] But the book's dust jacket romanticized its subjects as "America's newest power elite" and "urban explorers who are always in search of the 'perfect' CEO," and it described the executive search business as being "more lucrative than real estate, more unpredictable than the stock market."

In describing executive search consultants' penchant for Park Avenue (which today might be called the valley of the corporate kingmakers) and their unanimous demand for lavish working space, Byrne identified English foxhunting prints as "a nearly ubiquitous feature in headhunter offices." But some of the leading search consultants of the day also handed him ammunition to support their identity as headhunters.

Borrowing some executive recruiters' own words and adding some personal journalistic flourish, Byrne used no less than twelve different terms to label his book's central characters: *executive predators, deal makers, hired guns, executive searchers, executive hunter, business talent hunters, executive merchants, big-game hunters, executive headhunter, rainmaker, executive huntsman,* and even *executive hounds.* He quoted a variety of sources who added labels as paradoxical as *flesh peddler, corporate pariahs,* and *used car salesmen* on one hand, and *philosophy matcher* and *savior* on the other.

The book's descriptors for the day-to-day activities of these business consultants included "executive hunting," the "prowl for executives," "pirating," making "a body-snatching call," a "gentlemanly pursuit," a "mad scramble for business," and "the extremely competitive sport of corporate headhunting."

Frustrated as some were over Byrne's literary license, executive search consultants had no real right to hold a grudge, in part because of the lingo they used—and still use today—to describe their own work. Executive search consultants work with a hiring organization to develop a "job spec" that includes a list of sensible "target companies" from which to extract talent. They add to their deep and ever-growing candidate databases the names of talent-rich organizations whose people qualify for their "Most Wanted" lists. They also regularly engage in "shootouts" (dueling sales presentations) with other firms to win business.

Alternately belittling and exalting the business of executive search consulting and its best-known champions, Byrne wrote: "The business still lacks the credibility of the professions." He then quoted a chief executive who credited an executive search consultant with being "the main implement in helping us build the organization and bring in professional management," and establishing that "an executive headhunter can play a critical role in rejuvenating the management of a company."

Byrne's wasn't the first book to tackle the business, nor was it the last to trade on the pejorative. Legendary publisher Jim Kennedy's personal library included the following titles: *Secrets of a Corporate Headhunter, The New Secrets of a Corporate Headhunter,* and *Confessions of a Corporate Headhunter.* More recent additions to the literature of the field include *Headhunters Confidential, Headhunters Revealed,* and, introducing a candidate-focused perspective, *Be Hunted.*

TRANSACTION VS. STRATEGIC RECRUITMENT

One issue that seriously complicates the distinction between "executive search consultant" and "headhunter" is the existence of an entirely separate business of executive recruiters that embraces the pejorative. In the United States, for example, the oldest and largest market for executive recruiting services of any kind, two of every three executive search firms—or about four thousand of the nation's nearly six thousand—are contingency search firms. That is, they work on a contingent, nonexclusive basis for hiring organizations and get paid only if their work results in an actual hire by a searching employer.

These contingency headhunters, who have been known to define themselves as recruiting mercenaries, work almost entirely below the senior leadership level and take on assignments (sometimes along with other contingency search firms also hoping to produce the successful hire) for jobs that pay as little as $50,000 per year. They rarely see the $200,000-plus jobs, which hiring organizations generally entrust to an executive search consultant working on a retained, exclusive, and always confidential basis.

Without a mandate to analyze contenders for executive-level jobs in depth, contingency recruiters tend to interact with or otherwise respond to individuals whose résumés are easy to find. Any active jobseeker who has ever perused an online job board has likely seen the hordes of job opportunities posted by contingency recruiters hoping to generate a new round of candidate résumés. Retained executive search consulting firms have begun to post their own client job opportunities on niche professional- and executive-focused networking communities such as LinkedIn.com and ExecuNet.com, and on six-figure job sites such as BlueSteps.com, 6figurejobs.com, and Executivesontheweb.com. Contingency recruiters, however, post jobs on job boards in far greater numbers than retained firms, in part because there are more contingent-fee firms and they do a much higher volume of placements as a result of working below the division head and vice president levels.

Therein lies a key distinction between retained executive search consultants and contingency recruiters. The product offered by the vast majority of contingent-fee search work is an active job seeker, whereas that in a retained executive search assignment is almost always a gainfully employed and quite often sought-after executive who was effectively converted into a passive candidate for an executive position ranging from the manager level straight through to the "C-level" of for-profit and not-for-profit organizations.

The due diligence and time committed to filling a single management vacancy underscores the difference between recruiting talent on an exclusive basis (under which all or most of the fee is guaranteed) and recruiting talent on a contingency basis (under which pay is entirely contingent on placement, even if such a placement is billed in a retained fashion). It's also in many ways the difference between a consulting process and a sales transaction.

Another distinction between retained consultants and contingency headhunters is their earning power. For their work, a much higher percentage of which is conducted over the phone instead of in person, most contingency recruiters earn far less than executive search consultants. So the thought of becoming an executive search consultant is an inspiration for the contingency recruiter who wants to swim upstream in the management talent market.

The difference between a contingency headhunter and an "executive search consultant" may seem to resemble that between a salesperson and a "strategic accounts executive." It's certainly a matter of perspective. Nonetheless, it reveals much about the depth of a hiring organization's or job candidate's grasp of the situational context of their dialogue with these specialized management consultants.

Executive search consultants operate as corporate ambassadors, and they've often been described as "executive matchmakers" because they typically have just the right access to the caliber of senior management talent a hiring company desires. The matchmaking elements of executive recruiting and the experience she gained at a well-known search firm are what led Barbie Adler to drop out of executive search

Executive search consultants operate as corporate ambassadors, and they've often been described as "executive matchmakers."

in favor of her current job as founder and president of Selective Search, a boutique social matchmaking firm that touts "proven executive recruiting techniques" to "cherry-pick the must-meet women for our clients."

Adler, whose face has become known to many through her advertisements in airline in-flight magazines, succinctly captures some of the value points of executive search consulting in describing her current business: "Our clients have no problem dating, but they don't have the time, visibility or access to the caliber of woman they are looking to meet" for a personal relationship.[9]

THE NAYSAYERS

Some individuals and organizations malign executive search consultants in the hopes of one day replacing them. They covet executive recruiters' profit margins, their access to senior organizational leaders, and their influence over the world of business. Take the case of Jeff Hyman, who, as chief executive of upstart e-recruiting site Career Central Corp, predicted the impending unraveling (management consultants would call it "disintermediation") of the executive search consulting business.

Interviewed in the December 1, 1998, edition of *Inc.* magazine, Hyman boasted about his technology company's growth and said of executive search consultants, "They're middlemen on the verge of extinction. Those guys are gone. History. Toast. Stick a fork in 'em." You can be sure that Hyman long ago added those words to his "I Wish I Hadn't Said That" file. Just a few years later, he sold his company's assets—to, what else, an executive search consulting firm—and within several weeks departed to join another executive search firm.

Other like-minded technology types have also tried—and failed—to steal the business of the executive search consultant. Perhaps driven by the occasional business magazine cover featuring someone with the title of "CEO" who'd been recruited through an online job board, Monster.com launched ChiefMonster.com to facilitate a supposedly faster, better, cheaper way of recruiting top executive talent and knocking out executive search firms. Eventually, the ChiefMonster.com Web address unceremoniously redirected Web browsers to Monster.com.

WHAT'S IN A NAME?

Besides *headhunter,* a handful of other names can be used effectively to identify today's executive search consultant: *executive recruiter, management succession adviser,* and *corporate recruiting consultant.*

When the world's largest executive search consulting firms—two of which are publicly owned—were painfully reminded (after the dot-com collapse, the terrorist attacks of September 11, 2001, and the onset of a global recession) that their business of executive recruiting is tied closely to the business cycle, they moved quickly to diversify their portfolios of professional services before their shareholders realized the vulnerability.

Soon thereafter, those moves to diversify, besides adding a few new labels for executive recruiters, prompted the president of the Association of Executive Search Consultants to welcome its members to the meeting of what he jokingly described as the "Association of Non-Cyclical Business Services Providers." Two of the largest brand-name executive search firms subsequently went to market, respectively, as "leadership consultants" and "the premier provider of executive search, outsourced recruiting, and leadership development solutions."

"Headhunter" might aptly express a corporate HR executive's frustration with an executive recruiter who bungles a search process or fails to treat an executive job candidate with the utmost respect, candor, and discretion. And since most of the individuals who've received a call from an executive recruiter were never actually considered, interviewed, and placed as a result of the call, the pejorative may on the surface seem to fit. However, it fails to discriminate between specialized management consultants and those recruiting professionals who search for executive talent without an exclusive contract with hiring organizations.

The extent to which the word *headhunter* damages the image of management consultants who specialize in lining up top talent may really only become evident and be fully appreciated when one considers the issues in total. Taken in sum, it's easy to see how the very identity of the executive search consultant has become confused and distorted.

Simply put, the term *headhunter* is a politically incorrect pejorative that cheapens and serves to confuse the work of today's executive search consultant. It no longer fits in the twenty-first century. After all, how many hunters mean to do good for their quarry? "Headhunter" is a misnomer that, with others, has given a decidedly hard edge to a form of high-impact management consulting that today requires of its practitioners concern for how a career move is likely to affect families, judgment about recommending the candidate most deserving of the opportunity to lead, and cultural sensitivity (in both the organizational climate and inclusion-oriented senses) inside as well as outside the hiring organization. But practitioners of executive search first have to work much harder and more consistently to erase the pejorative and move the public and media labels of their work to something other than "headhunter" and "headhunting."

THE HEARTHUNTER

It is for all these reasons, coupled with the realization that even the most admirable executive search consultants must do a lot of work to prevent their being painted with the broad brush of headhunting, that I call up memories of my interactions with an exceptionally committed executive search consultant in Amsterdam.

This Dutch recruiter is passionate about serving the interests of his clients and being respectful of job candidates—as all great search consultants are—and that passion extends straight down the length of the blue, orange, and white scarf (adorned in the colors of his country's national flag) that he occasionally presents to people with whom he shares common interests and perspectives.

This is a man who understands the seriousness of his work. Who understands the tremendous influence he has on the future of companies and shareholders, whether they realize it or not. Who understands that executive search consulting is about serving the interests of organizations but also empathizing with the interests of transition-minded executives (and understanding the concerns and potential impact on a candidate's family or significant other). For at one end of the scarf he presents to friends and business associates is imprinted one word: *Hearthunter.*

In today's world, the heart matters as much as the head. Just consider the growing body of work around emotional intelligence—the recognition of how one person's behaviors and attitudes influence the behaviors and attitudes of others, and how it may be a better indicator of executive success than IQ. It's the recognition that one person can't do it all, that leadership means building and earning trust and motivating others. The world's best executive search consultants try to get a read not only on what's in a candidate's head but also on what's inside that candidate's heart and soul and how the whole person can boost or damage organizational esprit de corps and financial performance.

5

THE NEW LEADERSHIP MANDATE

Where does leadership begin? Where change begins.

JAMES MCGREGOR BURNS[1]

Driving down Interstate 95 in southern Connecticut, somewhere around Bridgeport, in the fall of 2006, motorists couldn't help reading a large billboard touting the reelection campaign then being mounted by the state's Fourth District congressman, Christopher Shays. What was striking about the billboard were the words used to describe the congressman's professed approach to serving his constituency: "Listens, Learns, Helps, Leads." No matter what your political persuasion, those words accurately and succinctly describe the true job requirements for today's corporate leaders and set a simple but high standard for future generations of business executives.

The words and the order in which they appeared on the billboard also speak directly to the concepts championed by the late pioneer of servant leadership Robert K. Greenleaf, a longtime AT&T executive who eventually became a noted author and scholar on the topic of leaders' choosing first to serve others. That campaign message obviously struck a chord with Connecticut voters on Election Day in November 2006. It was just enough for Shays to escape what amounted to a severe national backlash against the Republicans and their support of the U.S.-led war in Iraq.

Democrats won big in election races across New England, and when a Democratic challenger was declared the winner following a recount in another of Connecticut's congressional districts, Shays suddenly awoke to the realization that he would find himself the only Republican congressman from New England when the 110th Congress convened in January 2007.

Listens. Learns. Helps. Leads. Those words represented promises that Shays would have to put into practice to work effectively across party lines in the new, Democrat-controlled House of Representatives. They also prescribe a course of action for people in any organization who aspire to lead others. That's because leadership demands the kind of active listening that sharpens your perspective while honoring those who are given the opportunity to speak their mind. It demands that people learn enough from their mistakes to avoid repeating them. It demands that leaders be close to their followers and have both the courage and the humility to seek and practice forgiveness. And it demands all these so that you can lead yourself and others effectively.

"Leadership has the potential for doing serious meddling in the lives of others," says Larry C. Spears, executive director of the Greenleaf Center for Servant-Leadership, paraphrasing leadership author and consultant Max DePree.[2]

Executive search consultants are often agents of change for organizations, and it's when the future course of a company's strategy is at risk, under attack, or otherwise subject to uncertainty and doubt that the true value of managerial leadership reveals itself. The full courtship of senior management talent tells executive recruiters much about what they should be searching for, what they should be interviewing for, who they should recommend for leadership, and who among a short list of candidates should be dismissed from further consideration by the hiring organization.

"Leadership is a critical characteristic of an organization's success during the best of times," says John Murabito, executive vice president of human resources and services for CIGNA Corporation (NYSE: CI), a multibillion-dollar provider of health care and related benefits offered through the workplace. "During periods of change and transition it becomes the absolute critical element to an organization's ability to thrive. Courageous leadership is necessary."[3]

Now more than ever, says Chuck Bolton, president of Minneapolis-based executive development firm The Bolton Group and author of *Leadership Wipeout: The Story of an Executive's Crash and Rescue,* "organizations need a new, more authentic and enlightened leadership because the leader casts a long shadow across the organization."

THE FAILURE OF LEADERSHIP

"History has a way of matching man and moment." That's how George Herbert Walker Bush, speaking at the funeral of Gerald R. Ford, summed up the fate that brings leaders to the fore: It brought Abraham Lincoln to the challenge of the Civil War and the justice of the Emancipation Proclamation, and Winston Churchill and the whole world to the precipice of global tyranny during World War II. And it brought the man the first President Bush was then honoring, President Ford, to a decision about pardoning his disgraced predecessor, Richard M. Nixon.

The reins of organizational leadership also have a way of matching individuals to the challenges, risks, and opportunities of their times. Exceptional leaders are to be found in every walk of life, in every city, town, and village around the world. The world as we know it certainly couldn't be sustained without them. And people around the world will continue to rely on leadership—in all its forms, both known and mysterious—to support their very existence.

But if we've learned anything about organizational leadership in recent years, it's that the frailties of the human condition can set even the most accomplished, the best-known, and the highest-paid leaders on a collision course with history, social and organizational justice, and their own human failings. The scandals that have in recent years brought down some of the biggest and most powerful corporations and their leaders are proof of that and part of what's driving a call for better ethics, more effective corporate governance, and increased shareholder rights in business markets the world over.

The results released in December 2006 for the annual *USA Today*/Gallup poll measuring honesty and ethics in twenty-three occupations showed that only 2 percent of just over a thousand adult respondents gave business executives "very high" marks for honesty and ethical standards.[4] And those who know them best—their employees—question the basic morality of their organizations' top leaders and say that their managers do not treat them fairly, according to a separate survey of American workers.[5]

Only 18 percent of respondents to the *USA Today*/Gallup poll gave business executives "very high" or "high" ratings on ethics, down from 23 percent in 1999. That was on a par with the ratings given lawyers but only half the rating for chiropractors, one-third the ethics score for police officers, and one-fourth of the honesty tally for pharmacists, who ranked just below nurses (accorded the highest scores by 84 percent of respondents).

The occupations that scored lower than business executive when it came to judging honesty and ethics included U.S. senator, insurance salesperson, advertising practitioner, and car salesperson.

A postmortem on some of the scandals that have brought down powerful leaders in recent years reveals that a single common denominator often explains their behavior: greed. A Serbian proverb says, "A greedy father has thieves for children." And Mahatma Gandhi warned, "Earth provides enough to satisfy every man's need, but not every man's greed." Greed is one of the invisible character dynamics that can, and regularly does, influence executive decision making—and, by extension, the fates of customers, employees and their families, shareholders, and others whose salaries amount to a shrinking fraction of the compensation of the best-paid CEOs.

How else to explain many of the corporate scandals and other business news headlines of our times? Or the fact that, in the United Kingdom in recent years, the FTSE 100 chief executives have earned 98 times what the typical British worker has, or roughly two-and-a-half times the gap that insulated senior executives from their employees little more than five years earlier.

Those figures are especially appalling because they separate leaders from their followers, who are part of a global labor force the World Economic Forum has pegged at 3 billion people. The extraordinary sums paid to the world's chief executives could enrich many more lives if only they could be reallocated to others because, as Peter Singer, author of *One World: The Ethics of Globalization,* reminds us, at least "1.2 billion people in the world [are] living on $1 per day."

The new corporate leadership mandate requires that those who don the mantle of corporate authority grasp the need for corporate social responsibility, understanding, perhaps, that the global campaign against disease, hunger, and poverty remains humankind's biggest challenge.

EXECUTIVE RECRUITERS AS INFLUENCERS

The words of author and college student adviser Will Keim, one of the most dynamic speakers I've ever heard, come to mind as I consider the influence management recruiters could exert on the twisted mess that is executive compensation. Speaking of apathy and the need for more intervention to effect positive change in the world, Keim likes to remind audiences, "If you're not part of the solution, you're part of the problem." And those who influence CEO compensation are in a position to do the most to help.

It's painfully obvious that some of the highest-profile business leaders of our times appear to have been motivated by the quest for unprecedented personal wealth. Shareholders be damned! But it's high time that shareholders began to hold compensation committees and boards of directors accountable for giving their chosen executives golden hellos, golden handshakes, and golden parachutes galore.

It also may be time for those engaged in the recruitment of senior executives to begin interviewing and assessing candidates not only for their talents but also with an eye toward weeding out the greedy. Unfortunately, drilling down to identify a leadership candidate's real motivation for making a career move may be a tough task for search consultants, some of whom also measure their achievement by the size of their bank accounts and other personal assets.

Says retired search consultant Leon Farley, "Today's CEOs are facing, by and large, a pretty short life cycle. They don't expect to last. They expect to move on." But given the frequency of CEO and senior management firings and resignations, isn't it time for companies to take that shortening of the CEO employment cycle into consideration and let the air out of grossly inflated executive severance packages? After all, some of the record sums paid to CEOs would seem to express the hiring company's misplaced belief that this will be the chosen executive's last job—when, given the increase in CEO mobility, the company should be paying only for the kind of results it expects to achieve over the course of a few years.

CEOs' golden parachutes sometimes amount to hundreds of millions of dollars. It may not be the executive recruiters' job to control human greed, but it just might be their duty to the organizations they serve directly and to the shareholders and other stakeholders their clients ultimately must answer to. Part of the problem with executive compensation is that senior executives must set aside all but a few aspects of their personal life to tackle the requirements of the

Today's CEOs . . . don't expect to last. They expect to move on.

MEN WANTED

Men wanted for hazardous jouney.
Small wages. Bitter cold.
Long months of complete darkness.
Constant danger. Safe return doubtful.
Honour, and recognition in case of success.

never-ending job. For that sacrifice, executives want to be compensated handsomely. That is what seems to have opened the door to greed.

The arduous schedule and incredible demands faced by the CEO, in particular, have made the search—and the job specification—for today's chief executives akin to the recruitment notice reportedly published early in the twentieth century by South Pole explorer Sir Ernest Shackleton (with the exception, of course, of the "small wages").

The quest for organizational and individual excellence, taken together with companies' usual mismanagement of news about their executives' pay, add gasoline to the growing media spectacle and shareholder unrest about how corporate leaders' fortunes have become separated from those of the employees and shareholders they're supposed to serve.

Consider the case of Ford Motor Company's recruitment of CEO Alan Mulally from Boeing. This CNNMoney.com headline stoked Ford workers' ire: "Ford CEO: $28M for 4 months work."[6] The story, which detailed the contents of regulatory filings by the company, went on to explain how Ford, in the midst of a restructuring that closed plants and cut more than thirty thousand hourly positions to reduce losses, paid Mulally a $7.5 million hiring bonus, $11 million to offset forfeited performance and stock option awards from Boeing, and more than $55,000 in relocation expenses, plus stock grants, stock options, and his earned portion of what would be an annual base salary of $2 million.

Ford, which was then on the verge of losing to Toyota its longstanding number two ranking in U.S. auto sales, might have avoided such media coverage had it come clean at the time it recruited Mulally as president and CEO and offered a detailed outline of what it took to get him to leave his job as president and CEO of Boeing Commercial Airplanes. It could have then directly tied Mulally's compensation to the market demand for his services. But, instead, Ford delayed its public accounting of Mulally's pay package for several months, ultimately revealing the details in a proxy statement filed with the Securities and Exchange Commission and creating an immediate headache and perhaps a longer-term distraction for its chief executive.

CNNMoney.com's treatment of the story packed a punch, stating, "The company had disclosed in a footnote buried on page 228 of an earlier filing with the SEC that Mulally saw the value of his stock bonuses increase" and also outlining other goodies unveiled in the proxy statement, such as the personal use of company jets by Ford executives and the pay and flight costs racked up by executive chairman Bill Ford.

Executive recruiters occupy a unique position from which to intervene in, or at least to influence or advocate for a resolution of what many corporate customers and shareholders would describe as unreasonable executive compensation. So confident are executive search consultants about their ability to peer inside executive leadership candidates and render judgments about potential leaders that one mailed a holiday card with a cartoon on the front illustrating an executive search firm receptionist's guidance to an executive job candidate: "Mr. (Search Consultant) will see right through you now." If that is indeed the case, and given the many thousands of executives the typical search consultant interviews during the course of a working career, these consultants may be just the people to screen for executive malfeasance and financial motivation.

With more and more organizations demanding an informed outsider's read on executive leadership candidates' ethics, moral compass, and motivations, executive search consultants would be well advised to interview and assess for greed, and perhaps for other character flaws, not only as their duty but increasingly as their calling, and as a measure of the real value they bring to the process of recruiting top corporate management. Efforts along these lines may be behind the increasing popularity of behavior-based interviewing, which seeks to determine how executives would act in a given situation.

The true test of character is not how much we know how to do, but how we behave when we don't know what to do.

English jurist John Holt (1642–1709) said: "The true test of character is not how much we know how to do, but how we behave when we don't know what to do." The lesson for leadership recruiting: behavior is predictable, performance is not. So, these days more than a few executive recruiters like to ask about an executive's upbringing and social orientation, family life, personal life, and hobbies, and to gauge what this background might say about an executive's likely motivation to lead.

Executive recruiters bring a unique perspective to the judgment of executive leadership qualifiers because they see what many companies cannot see: the potential of external talent, how an executive's personal history might influence his or her decisions, and how the candidate's credentials might overcome organizational dysfunction and weaknesses that might not be apparent to insiders. One accomplished executive recruiter whose work is truly global in scope maintains that only a few questions need be considered with regard to a potential executive recruit:

Executive recruiters . . . see what many companies cannot see.

- Can the person do the job technically?
- Is the person recruitable? (That is, are there any compensation, legal, or family issues that would make hiring the person extremely difficult or unlikely?)
- Is there a chemistry fit between the executive and the potential employer?
- Is there full organizational awareness of what's necessary to include in or exclude from the offer, the job title and responsibilities, and the compensation package?
- How did the person score on any assessment tests that were administered?

Another deeply experienced recruiter (who cut his teeth in management consulting) says the challenge of sorting out the right candidate boils down to matching qualifications to the job spec or mandate:

- What are the near-term objectives of the organization and the role?
- What problems or hurdles must be overcome?

- What kinds of skills and background experiences are required to overcome them?
- What is the strategic value of leadership in this role?
- From an organizational culture angle, what does it take to succeed in this environment?

Executive search consultants face the challenge of facilitating a discreet, often ultra-urgent courtship and committal process that requires the gradual engagement of client and candidate and the mitigation of risk for both parties. That challenge makes these questions especially relevant. To the checklists just presented, one might add this question:

- How much does the prospect regard as appropriate to be paid over the next year, two years, and perhaps even three years if the performance expectations spelled out in the job specification (and any additional responsibilities added later) are met or exceeded?

The answer to this question may reveal something about the executive's motivation, as will the closing negotiations between a transition-minded business executive and a hiring organization that's convinced of the candidate's qualifications. That deal-closing process usually also tells the search consultant much about the motivation of both parties.

But it's also clear that shareholders, board members, and financial analysts need a common scorecard with which to evaluate the performance of a chief executive, much in the same way a baseball player's batting average, on-base percentage, slugging average, runs batted in, and games played all factor in to set the fair market value for that player.

WHAT LEADERSHIP ALWAYS LOOKS LIKE

The words of the Scout Law, twelve simple adjectives describing the character traits expected to develop within all Boy Scouts, go a long way toward prescribing the things hiring organizations and their leadership talent scouts—the executive search consultants—should expect of all leaders, whether in senior corporate management, government, politics, or other walk of life:

> *A Scout is trustworthy, loyal, helpful, friendly, courteous, kind, obedient, cheerful, thrifty, brave, clean, and reverent.*"

Funny how some of the best guidance for leading—and deciding who leads—comes to us when we're young and perhaps not old enough to fully appreciate the lesson and meaning.

Rodman L. Drake, a former strategy consultant who sits on the boards of a handful of public and private companies, once framed the demands of corporate leadership and specifically the CEO role this way: "The successful CEO changes the direction of an enterprise and gets it to move toward his vision. A CEO brings about change through a complex combination of building support and consensus, sequencing decisions, decreasing uncertainty through better-quality information and developing an acute sense of timing."[7]

Also consider the ways in which the emotional intelligence quotient, or EQ—perhaps even more than traditional IQ—has become something of a baseline from which recruiters might judge an individual's fitness for leadership. True leaders exhibit high emotional intelligence, which helps them understand how their behavior, their decisions, and their example influence the attitudes, work, performance, and lives of many others around them, as well as of people in consumer markets and business units often spread across the globe. EQ is indeed an effective measure of executive leadership competency.

Jack Lowe Jr., the CEO of Dallas-based TD Industries (now included in *Fortune* magazine's "100 Best Companies to Work for in America" Hall of Fame) and himself a past recipient of the National Ernst & Young Entrepreneur of the Year Award for Principle-Centered Leadership, was right when he said, "Leadership includes courage and risk-taking. . . . It's dangerous, sometimes lonely work."[8] It also can be thankless work. Some of the best examples come in the form of everyday leadership. This is leadership we often fail to recognize—leadership that humbles righteous people when they see it or feel its loving touch. It's evident in leaders like these:

- The parish priest who listens to humanity's transgressions and then goes about treating people the same way he did before he learned of their sins
- The small business owner who honors employees by asking them to share something of themselves—be it personal or professional—at each staff meeting, so they feel more a part of a job and team that require much of their time and energy each week
- The university professor who teaches forgiveness and, in so doing, asks for it, also daring others to forgive
- The single mother of two young children who donates $1,000 to charity before Christmas because she wants to teach her kids about kindness to others even though she finds it hard to make ends meet
- The preschool teachers who love young children and who offer (and learn) many lessons about human behavior, but whose work is underappreciated and woefully undercompensated
- The immigrant auto dealership employee whose hard work, commitment to his job, and positive attitude make him a leader in the eyes of other, much more highly compensated employees who admire his determination to build a future for his family
- The social services worker who gives much of herself to care for the physically and mentally challenged and who, for her sacrifice of service, is often left struggling to pay her family's bills

Some authors and researchers have surmised from their interviews and experiences that in order to be granted the opportunity to lead others from an executive management post, including that of CEO, one must be male, tall, good-looking, and married for thirty years to the same wife. Those things certainly won't work against you. And yet, despite some compelling anecdotal evidence that the loyalty, support, care, nurturing, and compassion that's required of long-married people may transfer well to the stewardship of an organization, leadership takes many forms and isn't the sole domain of people who may convince themselves that they deserve the reins of leadership for anything other than performance-based reasons.

No matter what their background, appearance, academic record, or social standing, leaders share credit, acknowledge their mistakes, and commit to team play. They have a well-checked (if not quiet and understated) self-confidence, character, and sense of competence. They must know themselves well—including their faults—and know others well if they are to communicate corporate strategy effectively and in a way that demonstrates how others' performance helps achieve organizational objectives. Table 2 lists the main demands on a leader.

TABLE 2 **Requisite Leader Attributes**

Callings		**Essentials**	
Trust builder	Confidant	Integrity	Service orientation
Good example	Mentor	Vision	Stewardship
Steward	Inventor	Cultural sensitivity	Life balance
Team captain	Artful reinventor	Positive attitude	Leadership development
Cheerleader	Corporate citizen	Enthusiasm	Fairness
Coach	Beacon of hope	Visibility	
Referee	Motivator	Courage	
Team player	Inspirer	Self-knowledge	
Advocate	Calculated risk taker	Communication skills	
Lifelong learner			

The word *friend* may also belong on the list of leadership callings. Although most employers value leaders who bring to their role a sense of urgency, a growth mind-set, decisiveness, and a compelling vision for change plus the courage to make it happen (and to learn from an occasional mistake), the best leaders endeavor to serve and satisfy all their constituents, knowing full well that even their best efforts may still fall short of making everyone happy.

Some may disagree with the *friend* bit, but consider what the *Harvard Business Review* has said about organizational coaching: "We have not seen a company that can't benefit from more candor, less denial, richer communication, conscious development of talent and disciplined leaders who show compassion for people."[9]

Effective communication can't be overstated as a key to leadership and, for that matter, to leadership recruiting. So says Deborah Dumaine, author of *Write to the Top: Writing for Corporate Success* and president of Better Communications, a global learning and consulting firm that helps organizations become more productive and profitable through improved writing. "Businesses have looked under every rock looking for efficiencies in technology, supply chain, or operations. But most haven't recognized that the next frontier is right in their in-box," Dumaine says. "Trends in telecommuting and decentralization dictate that we all must rely on the written word to get things done: the need is at every level from leadership to today's emerging, multilingual workforce." And as the massive Baby Boomer generation retires from workforces around the world, she adds, "Companies will face a dramatic labor shortage of people with functional writing skills—to say nothing of leadership-level writing. Corporate survival will depend on transforming practices to develop all levels of employees. Only the fittest communicators will compete successfully."

It's the communication and meaningful expression of goodwill, the earnest concern for one's constituencies, and the candor, compassion, and hard work that come with the job that, collectively, contribute to what has become known as servant leadership. The doctrine of servant leadership suggests that it is incumbent on leaders to demonstrate compassion for and connectivity with their teams. That effort communicates genuine concern for others. Leaders lead by example and put themselves in a position to earn the trust and respect of others who share (or who eventually may share) the same organizational objective. That's critical, especially when leaders must ask their followers to take on more responsibility or otherwise contribute something more of themselves for the greater good.

Authority is not a license to treat people poorly. In fact, authority—like leadership in general—requires that people go out of their way to treat people, be they customers, employees, or shareholders, courteously and kindly, even those who are confused, in the wrong, or simply uninformed.

There is much people can learn from each other, and that potential conjures a passage from the Bible, from Proverbs 29, that I heard from a thoughtful Gonzaga University classmate: "Like iron on iron, one man sharpens another." Leaders can't try to change or improve an organization, or, given the rising concerns about corporate social responsibility, the environment, and child and slave labor, try to change the world without taking time to get to know it through the eyes of other people.

Humankind's biggest challenges remain the global blight of hunger, disease, and dire poverty that mires families in a cycle of intolerable work conditions, malnutrition, and lack of education, and the leaders of the future won't really be leaders at all unless they and their organizations are doing something about it. Here is a to-do list for a leader in the twenty-first century:

- Become emotionally connected with your people but take emotion out of hard decisions.
- Master the details without getting entangled in them.
- Grasp opportunity to influence others and know how you should and shouldn't be influenced.
- Learn from mistakes but acknowledge that future decisions will include other missteps.
- Embrace the art of genuine apology and know when and how to practice it.
- Spread organizational passion and momentum and be accountable for changes in course.

- Develop a reputation for toughness and fairness.
- Make a good first impression with employees and customers and build lasting impressions.
- Lead by example and understand how it affects the motivation and behavior of others.
- Give others the opportunity to lead and learn more about what inspires followers.

THE WAY FORWARD

The confluence of globalization and technology with increasing consumer demands, environmental concerns, scrutiny on effective governance and ethics, and calls for corporate social responsibility is pressuring corporate leaders as never before. It is also ratcheting up the pressure on executive search consultants.

In many industries, consolidation options are scant at best, and the prospect of raising prices to meet the growth that shareholders expect is becoming less viable as increasingly value-conscious consumers follow deals and price breaks seemingly wherever they can find them.

In human capital terms, the new global economy demands that executives be accountable. It demands that directors invest the time to serve as effective stewards of shareholder confidence. It demands that corporate executive staffing teams and executive search consultants tap a global talent market, and that workers at every level of the organization do their fair share to optimize corporate performance.

These new challenges bring with them hugely inflated expectations of corporate senior management. Most of them demand massive doses of organizational change, which has only fueled demand for external executive search, and, in the words of one newspaper headline, heralds the advent of an era in which "outsiders [are] gaining the inside track for CEO positions."[10]

Decisions about who should lead an organization are almost always made by people in positions of power above that of the individual who will be appointed as leader. In a search for an outside director, it's the current board members. In a CEO search, it's again the board, probably acting in a more formal, ceremonial, and committee-driven process. At the vice president level, it's typically the CEO. At each of these levels, many draw on the help of an executive search consultant, who brings a valuable outside perspective.

But the best decisions about leadership are made with input from those who will report to the new leader because workers often have much to say about what they've witnessed, how they feel about where the organization is heading, and which inside candidates have earned their respect. Servant leaders know to ask for advice, listen intently to it, and in the process, pay respect to employees and come away with a more informed view of what must be decided. Today's leading organizations, be they for-profit companies, nonprofit organizations, governments, or educational institutions, must realize the need to become entirely multicultural, multigenerational, and fair in terms of deciding who will lead, who will set the organization's compass, and who will establish and guide its employment culture and experience.

Today's leaders must surround themselves with the best and brightest management executives and then act to develop and retain them, in part because it has become both an organizational and a career mandate. Just ask Phil Purcell, former CEO of Morgan Stanley, whose resignation was both trumpeted and explained by a *USA Today* headline: "Mass Exodus by Morgan Stanley Execs Leads to CEO's Resignation."[11]

Leaders must have an acute sense of how their actions and their failure to act affects others who work with and for them or are served by their products and services. Emotional intelligence is all about measuring one's decisions and judgments by assessing their impact on the larger community, perhaps even the world. "Leadership should be born out of the understanding of the needs of those who would be affected by it," as singer Marian Anderson (1902–1993) said.

It is the responsibility of leaders to drive their competitive advantage through human capital. Competitors can copy strategy and technology, but they cannot copy an organization's people and their rules of engagement with customers, with management, and with others, or the way talented people work toward common goals.

The growing influence of manufacturing excellence concepts like Six Sigma and Lean on modern-day approaches to corporate management calls increasingly for leaders who can master the process of change with a near zero-defect result. Supply chain management best practices are beginning to influence recruiting and talent management best practices.

The best leaders are some of the best recruiters because they understand how a positive attitude, raw talent and determination, cultural sensitivity, and a willingness to respect and learn from others can help individuals overcome almost anything to achieve great things for themselves and those around them. "You're only as good as the people who work for you," a then seventy-seven-year-old coworker once reminded me.

"The best leader," Theodore Roosevelt said, "is the one who has sense enough to pick good men to do what he wants done, and the self-restraint to keep from meddling with them while they do it." When a true leader is surrounded by good people, the possibilities are endless. An advertising billboard in one of the terminals at Chicago's O'Hare International Airport once read: "Success is the sum of the confident decisions you make." To that, one might add, "about your executive recruiting."

You're only as good as the people who work for you.

6

THE TRUE COST OF A BAD EXECUTIVE HIRE

The higher up in the organization, the more breakage is likely to occur.

JAMES P. MOONEY, SVP AND SENIOR CONSULTANT, FARR ASSOCIATES

If companies calculated the total cost of bad executive recruitment decisions—and the organizational breakage that ensues—they would surely work much more diligently to prevent them and to partner effectively with executive search consultants. They would do whatever it takes to increase the probability that the new leader will fit, stay, and succeed with the company. They would train their management in effective interviewing and leadership assessment, and they would provide effective onboarding programs. They would also evaluate how their current recruiting processes and engagement of executive search consulting firms contribute to the problem and the solution.

Part of the justification for hiring an executive search consultant is the realization that an organization can't afford to recruit the wrong person and isn't willing to settle for second best. When companies place a significant bet on the wrong senior leadership candidate from inside or outside the organization, or, for that matter, on the wrong search consultant, the total cost of that misfit executive hire can be huge, and also especially hard to calculate in full. That's because at the executive management level, poor recruiting and hiring decisions can lead to an embarrassing and potentially very public dismissal or resignation of a key executive—and often the team of lieutenants the newcomer may in turn have recruited from the outside.

More important, a bad executive hire can also trigger cultural tremors whose shock waves reverberate throughout a division, office, or specific business unit or, worse, throughout the entire organization and beyond, to the shareholders, analysts, and media. And a bad executive hire, unlike a mistake made farther down the organization chart, can create unwanted anxiety, drama, and distraction among employees and fuel an increase in management turnover at all levels. The true cost must be tallied in time and opportunity lost, organizational resources expended, and harm done to organizational morale, productivity, and reputation, a disaster that may require a long-term organizational recovery process. Its effects should not be underestimated or ignored. It simply doesn't take long for the wrong executive to lose your company a lot of money.

It simply doesn't take long for the wrong executive to lose your company a lot of money.

Take the case of a well-known, widely respected, and financially solvent health care institution that recruited a new CEO, who in turn recruited a number of management-level employees to serve as his lieutenants, but who, unbeknownst to his new employer, had left two previous employers in poor financial condition. By the time the institution recognized the CEO's incompetence, it was already too late.

The hundreds of thousands of dollars spent on executive search fees were only the start. The institution ultimately racked up almost $65 million in losses in the final year of the CEO's nearly three-year tenure, besides what it cost to extricate him (and presumably others he brought in) from the organization and to pay the legal fees incurred as a result of this executive recruiting calamity. The trickle-down effects of poor recruitment and reference-checking decisions on the part of the institution and its chosen search firm carried a huge price tag—not only because the new CEO was the wrong person for the top job but also because he used his position to alter the strategy and culture of the organization.

DIAGNOSING ORGANIZATIONAL BREAKAGE

Even before the hiring organization realizes it has a problem with an executive-level recruit, the cost of the individual's misalignment with the enterprise, its people, and its strategic objectives begins to add up.

Just getting to the point of making a decision about intervention can be time-consuming and uncomfortable. Actual intervention only exacerbates the institutional discomfort, which may explain why so many employers wait until there's trouble—financial, cultural, or otherwise—before they do anything to address the problem and make a difficult change in senior management leadership. By that time, the misfit executive may have exacted a toll on the organization's people, some of whom may never recover to their full potential or even to past performance levels because of their loss of faith in the organization and its leadership selection criteria, or its lack thereof.

Says James P. Mooney, a senior consultant with leadership consultancy Farr Associates, which was founded in 1956 in High Point, North Carolina: "If this [individual] is not going to work out, the painful process of getting to that decision point is likely to create a lot of breakage. The people he or she interacts with will form camps and retreat into their silos. Some people may leave—and we know the good ones leave first. And the higher up in the organization, the more breakage is likely to occur, and the deeper will be the cracks in the organization the next placement will need to heal."

While the impact of a bad executive hire on an organization can be enormous, it's important to point out that a leadership recruiter's simple mismatch of an individual and an employer can also cause significant damage to the career and reputation of the executive concerned. However, neither the executive nor the executive search consultant should consider a mismatch a fatal or career-ending experience, unless it emerges as or contributes to a pattern of misalignment with employers or clients. Much in the same way that great leaders occasionally make bad decisions, so do executive search consultants inadvertently (but if they're top-notch, very infrequently) introduce a client employer to a prospective recruit who just won't fit with the organization's cultural fabric.

The ultimate dismissal or resignation of an externally recruited business leader is itself a stinging rebuke of the search consultant (unless the hiring organization failed to support and onboard the new executive). But the occasional recruitment misstep reminds many recruiters of the need for constant due diligence when it comes to client employers and their shifting strategic challenges and resulting leadership requirements.

Executive search consultants are paid to introduce candidates who bring a unique shape or puzzle piece to the hiring organization's cultural, social, and political mosaic. They sit in judgment of personality, communication and leadership styles, past performance, and a slate of intangibles that give them confidence—or lack of confidence—in how a particular executive might meet a client's test of leadership. And sometimes they get it wrong, perhaps because of their rush to judgment or due to human factors outside their control.

Search consultants like to point to their long-term contribution to client employers as measured through the tenure, performance, and promotion of key executives they've recruited, although scant few have invested the time and energy to benchmark those placement metrics. Any anomaly in their client work stands out like a sore thumb and skews the measurement of their performance and impact for the hiring organization, so employers can be sure that their search consultants are as wary as they are about choosing the wrong person for a senior management position.

The impact of each leadership recruitment and selection decision, however, is most consequential for the hiring organization itself, measured in innumerable ways by the potential upside of a great choice, and the potential breakage caused by a poor choice. It's also consequential for the recruit's former employer. Consider the defection or seduction of an especially talented software engineer, pharmaceutical scientist, fund manager, or chief marketing officer and how much their respective efforts mean to product development, drug discovery, total shareholder returns, and new business development. The disruption to personnel, operations, and research and development initiatives can put a significant crimp in profits and the attainment of business continuity and strategic planning objectives.

CALCULATING THE COST

Estimates of the cost of a bad executive hire have ranged from three to five times the misfit executive's annual salary up to hundreds of times the value of that same six-figure management salary. The cost can't be computed in the abstract, by some magic formula, because all organizations are different, the challenges they present are unique, and the quality of the resource they increasingly feed on—senior leadership talent—runs the gamut of human individuality. Nonetheless, it is possible to deconstruct the process that led to the recruiting misfire and calculate the costs incurred in recognizing the problem, dealing with it, and restocking the team with a new leader or key executive-level contributor. The decision to hire the wrong person has direct costs (the sunk costs or wasted institutional resources that are easiest to measure) and indirect costs (which are both more significant and more difficult to recognize and account for).

PepsiCo, which for some time has been more sophisticated than most large companies about understanding the impact of great leadership recruiting and the cost of poor hiring decisions, calculated the cost of a bad executive hire at $250,000 in the late 1990s. The company also found that an 87 percent reduction in the turnover of executives at that replacement cost saved it $5.4 million.[1] For Mobil Corporation, a forerunner to ExxonMobil (the world's largest company), the assignment of a poorly chosen executive to work in the Middle East was calculated to cost $375,000.[2]

What far too many companies fail to realize, however, is that the full direct costs of a bad executive hire typically amount to between two and three times that individual's annual salary, and that this figure accounts for only 20 percent of the total damage done to the organization's performance. The indirect impact—measured in reduced performance, opportunity cost, energy and resources wasted, and goodwill squandered—combine to cost the organization between eight and twelve times the misfit executive's annual salary. These indirect costs amount to the other 80 percent of the toll a bad executive hire takes on organizational performance.

The direct costs of a bad executive hire account for only 20 percent of the total damage done to the organization's performance.

Direct Costs

Direct costs or wasted resources from a bad executive hire include these elements:

- **The cost of the executive's initial recruitment and total compensation.** This figure includes salary, bonuses, stock awards, and benefits, plus all the fees paid to a search consultant (typically one-third of the first year's salary and bonus), compensation consultant, and background or reference checking firm, as well as any relocation expenses and legal fees.
- **The cost of extraction, or removing the executive.** These costs include guaranteed severance pay and any legal fees incurred.
- **The cost of replacing the misfit executive.** Included in this amount are at least the expenses for a replacement search or the fee charged by a new search firm, the money paid to other consultants (perhaps now including an onboarding expert if the hiring company has gotten smart about its recruiting process), and possibly the cost of relocating and paying an interim executive charged with handling the role until the permanent replacement can take charge.

The problem for most organizations is that they fail to track executive recruitment effectiveness and the cost of their bad leadership hires. And they should realize that, although a search consultant may be accountable for conducting a replacement search for "expenses only," the true costs the organization will incur as a result of a poor leadership selection decision stretch far beyond the executive recruiter's invoices.

Indirect Costs

The indirect costs that result from a bad executive management hire include these factors:

- **Disruption of unit performance and customer relationships.** The period before, during, and immediately after the organization recognizes that the executive is not a good fit, extracts the executive, and prepares to find a successor is fraught with chaos. The impact on revenue, profit, and total returns to shareholders can be significant. And, as one leadership consultant acknowledges, the process can create "a more difficult change path for the next placement, with barriers we could have avoided."
- **Loss of unit and leadership productivity.** Such a loss is especially prevalent while a search for a replacement is being conducted. The average executive search takes about four months, but the time involved hinges on availability of candidates sourced during the original search assignment. The time it takes for a new executive to join and integrate or onboard into the organization, adapt to the new environment, and learn what's really required of the role poses additional opportunity cost.
- **Loss of potential opportunities.** Especially hard to calculate, this cost is enormous. It can be measured in the loss of organizational momentum toward achieving strategic objectives, loss

of market opportunities, loss of market share to competitors, and investments made in support of the departed executive's misaligned priorities. This particular performance impact grows substantially if exceptionally qualified runners-up to the original search process are no longer available or have assumed leadership roles with the competition.

- **Management-level churn and turmoil.** There can be a very serious and potentially huge cost (both financial and cultural) of dismissing and replacing other management-level employees, who were recruited because of their particular synergy with the interests of the now-departed executive.
- **Loss of goodwill with high-performing employees.** The specter of the misfit executive's burning the organization's goodwill with high-performing employees looms large. This loss could lead to a drop in morale, motivation, productivity, overall employee engagement, satisfaction, and retention. This is especially germane if the drama surrounding the hiring and eventual firing of the misfit executive leads to a widespread loss of confidence and trust within the organization. Such a loss could snowball into the departure of other key executives, who will take their intellectual capital, networks, and relationships with them, along with some important institutional knowledge.

Thus indirect costs of a bad executive hire include "the potential damage to the reputation of the company and its board, the amount of time officers and directors will have to spend correcting the mistake, the postponement of major decisions awaiting a new leader, any damages done by the former executive, and the marginalization of key executives who were not chosen and may have left the company to seek greener pastures," says Durant A. "Andy" Hunter, managing partner of leadership consultancy Ridgeway Partners. "Meanwhile," he adds, "the competition is moving forward." Figure 1 captures all these costs in graphic form.

FIGURE 1 **Deconstructing the Total Cost of a Bad Executive Hire**

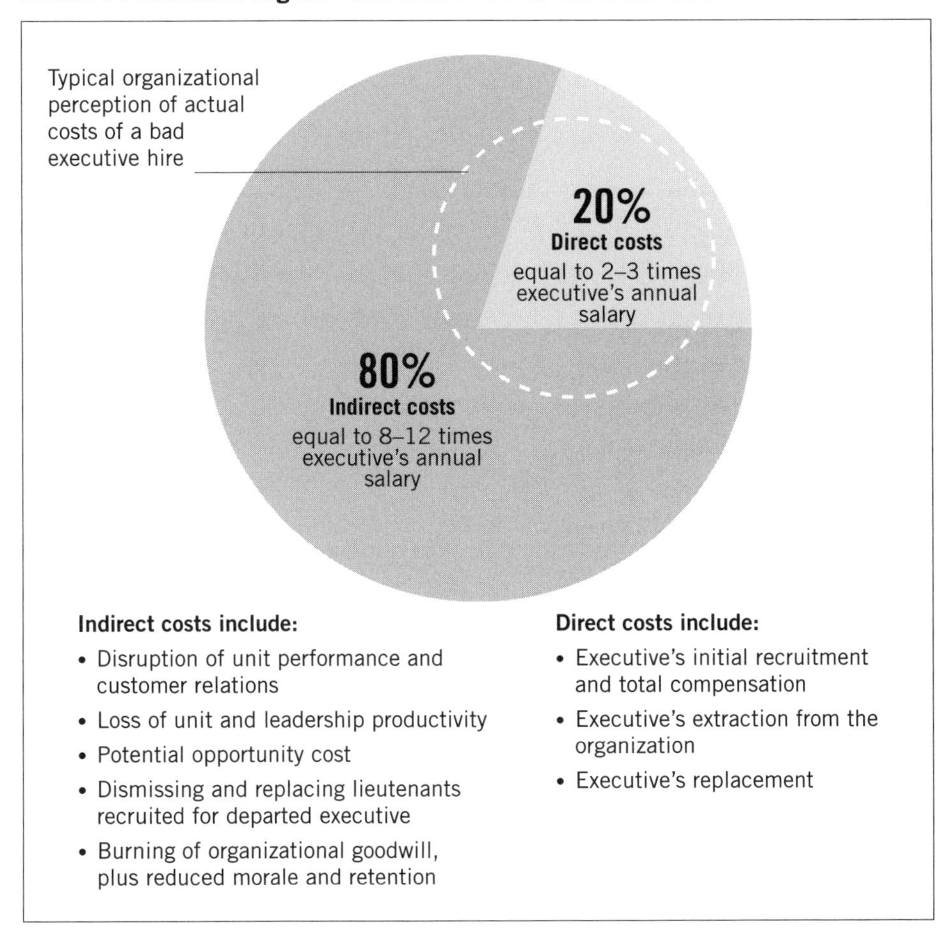

The higher up the organizational hierarchy a mishap occurs, the higher the cost. The cost of hiring the wrong C-suite executive can debilitate an organization, especially one that ranks somewhere outside the Fortune 500 or the Forbes Global 2,000 largest employers. "True, executive search is widely accepted by the corporate giants," executive search publisher Jim Kennedy once wrote, "but it's even more important for smaller companies, where one hiring mistake can have disastrous results."

In particular, the misadventure of hiring the wrong CEO or CFO candidate from outside brings significant risk in terms of potential public relations nightmares, a crisis of confidence among shareholders and employees, increased legal liability, and regulatory and governance interventions.

Worse still, the individual reputation of the fired CEO or CFO can begin to migrate onto the organization's unique brand, thereby creating consumer confusion and potentially a significant loss of market share and earnings. This happens because these executives are personally accountable for financial reporting. If the media covering the dismissal dwell on embarrassing circumstances leading up to it, people will associate the company with the fired executive.

[Executive search is] even more important for smaller companies, where one hiring mistake can have disastrous results.

That kind of association in the minds of consumers around the world can lead to loss of market share and brand awareness as well as the diminution of corporate reputation and long-term total returns to shareholders. Just consider for a moment the public's direct and lingering association between the names of convicted businessmen L. Dennis Kozlowski and Jeffrey Skilling and the names of the companies they once led—Tyco International Ltd. and Enron, respectively.

Leadership consultant Andy Hunter says, "Hiring is always a gamble. The trick is to improve the odds. The soundest way to improve the odds is to make sure the chemistry is right for both parties." So what can hiring organizations do to minimize the risk of making a costly executive hiring mistake? Here are the tips Hunter offers for minimizing the inherent risks of executive recruiting:

- **Make sure the goals and objectives of the position are clear and achievable.** If you don't know what you are looking for, anyone will do! Make sure your whole organization, or at least anyone involved in the interview process, has a degree of consistency. Good candidates look for clarity, a sound business model, and the alignment of interests between the board and management.

- **Assess the candidate's abilities in terms of realistic expectations and in terms of the most important tasks to be achieved.** Too often, discussions about a candidate's suitability get sidetracked, leading to poor hiring decisions. With the job correctly scoped, you will be better equipped to determine whether the person can do the job.
- **Understand the candidate's motivation.** What is driving the candidate? Is that motivator compatible with your organization? Also, is the candidate's leadership style compatible with the company and its employees? Communication skills, body language, humor, and style are important and need to be incorporated into the hiring decision.
- **Reference, reference, reference.** Hire a third party, not the search firm, to conduct reference checks. Get as many snapshots from different angles as possible. Does the executive have the collaborative skills to work with the talent at hand? Is the executive flexible, willing to listen and take suggestions?

After considering these four guidelines, Hunter says, it's important to consider one last piece of advice, something about assessing talent that he learned from a client early in his consulting career: Is the candidate "a 'scorer' or a 'skater'?" As Hunter explains it, "Skaters suit up well, work hard, but can't find the net. The client wanted a scorer . . . a leader, someone who would make a real difference. If you are looking for winners and want to reduce the risk, separate the scorers from the skaters."

Hiring is always a gamble. The soundest way to improve the odds is to make sure the chemistry is right for both parties.

7

THE INTERSECTION OF EXECUTIVE SEARCH AND EXECUTIVE ONBOARDING

> You never get a second chance to make a good first impression.
>
> **UNKNOWN**

If you want senior management executives to contribute faster, perform better, and stay longer, make a commitment to get them started well in their new leadership role.

Other than an executive search consultant's guarantee on the tenure of an externally recruited executive, corporate employers can have no better protection for their investment in the executive search than an effective transition, integration, or onboarding program that will help newly hired executives chart and begin to tackle strategically aligned priorities and safeguard their early performance. That's very important, considering the growing corporate impatience for results and the sink-or-swim mentality about executive integration that has permeated business for many decades, as evidenced by this stark admission from the head of human resources for a major global employer: "We've done a world-class awful job of getting people started."

It's no wonder that as many as 40 percent of new executive hires fail within their first eighteen months on the job, and that, according to

ExecuNet research, more than one-third of companies are moving to stamp out executive transition casualties by providing coaching or other onboarding assistance for their newly recruited or promoted executives.[1]

A compelling business case can be made for organizations to invest in the smooth landing and effective transition of their executive talent. After all, recruiting a new executive is an expensive proposition, as fees and expenses for a retained executive search often exceed 33 percent of the recruited executive's first-year total compensation. At the same time, the success rate in retaining external management hires is poor, with some organizations revealing in surveys and anecdotally that the turnover rate among their external executive leadership hires runs between 20 percent and 40 percent. Such a continuous and staggering cycle of recruiting, training, and replacing misfit executives can hurt an organization's bottom line, impinge on employee morale and engagement, and reduce not only productivity but total returns to shareholders.

We've done a world-class awful job of getting people started.

When the Corporate Leadership Council, a Washington, D.C.–based research firm, looked at why executives fail in new leadership roles, failure to build meaningful working partnerships with peers and subordinates ranked at the top of the list (82 percent), followed by lack of clarity or confusion about role expectations (58 percent), lack of political savvy (50 percent), failure to achieve two or three critical expected objectives (47 percent), and taking too long to learn (28 percent).[2]

Another perspective on the challenges of onboarding is revealed in the results of a three-year study by Leadership IQ, a leadership training and research company also based in Washington, D.C. Leadership IQ polled 5,247 hiring managers from 312 public, private, business, and health care organizations, who collectively hired more than twenty thousand employees during the study period. The study found that 26 percent of new hires fail because they can't accept feedback, 23 percent because they're unable to understand and manage emotions, 17 percent because they lack the necessary motivation to excel, 15 percent because they have the wrong temperament for the job, and only 11 percent because they lack the necessary technical skills.[3]

"Lack of technical skills is not why people are failing," says Mark Murphy, chairman and CEO of Leadership IQ. "It's their lack of coachability, their emotional intelligence, their temperament, and the speed and intensity of challenges they face." The sheer pressure to perform is mounting earlier in a new executive's tenure than ever before, and the hiring organization bears great responsibility not only for supporting a leader's job transition but for ensuring that its candidate interviewing process leads it to the right person in the first place.

The key interpersonal traits turn out to be the ones that are the most difficult to interview for. They also take the most time to train others to interview for, and, Murphy adds, many corporate recruiters lack the incentive to take the necessary time to truly understand them as they relate to organizational management needs.

THE CASE FOR ONBOARDING

Onboarding, as the name implies, constitutes a learning exercise of coaching and performance feedback appraisals executed soon after a management job offer is accepted, soon after an executive's start date—perhaps 90, 100, or 120 days into someone's tenure in a new leadership post—or both. Research by RHR International, a leader in executive and organizational development, suggests that full integration takes between twelve and eighteen months as the executive moves (and faces new challenges) through four stages of integration, from honeymoon to reality to adjustment and then, finally, to full integration.

Whatever its form and duration, the move from executive onboarding to full integration comes at the employers' expense, and increasingly, it's being built into or offered in tandem with the executive search process. It is also a potentially career-saving measure that smart executives, over time, will learn to demand as they negotiate their new salary and benefits package.

Onboarding (and similar programs executed under more awkward labels such as *management integration, alignment,* and *assimilation coaching,* to name a few) informs a new executive's perspectives about the new employer's workplace culture, corporate strategy, key influencers and decision makers, productivity traps, and early identifiable wins. It goes beyond mere orientation, giving the executive valuable feedback about perceived strengths and weaknesses from a variety of constituencies, perhaps including the board, the CEO, key shareholders, executive peers, and subordinates.

The intent is to help new executives gauge the organization's early read on their management style, rectify any problems or misconceptions about their intentions and priorities, and otherwise accelerate progress on strategic goals that are aligned with the interests of the board, the CEO, and other key stakeholders, and with their own performance assessment milestones. Of course, the outcome depends on what new executives then choose to do with that information and level of support they get from their new employer to put plans into action. At best, onboarding quickly establishes institutional and social goodwill that the executive leader can ultimately spend toward gaining support for organizational change.

"In general, the process sends a good message," says B. Simone Caruthers, senior consultant and psychologist with Farr Associates, which supports the transition of senior corporate leaders. Soliciting feedback from peers, superiors, and subordinates through onboarding surveys sends a positive message, she says: "I want to know how I am doing, and your feedback matters." Caruthers adds: "It is not unusual for the recruited person to be [someone] who has had to make changes. This can be threatening to people who are impacted by the change. The survey sends a message that the new person may not be totally uncaring. However, the follow-up after the survey is the crucial part. It is often a useful way for the recruited person to connect with people."

An executive hired to be an agent of significant change or perhaps to orchestrate a cultural transformation of the organization must fully understand its current organizational identity—from inside and outside points of view—in order to conceptualize, evangelize, and execute the move toward a new strategic destination. However, too many organizations around the world fail to make sure that a new executive is smoothly introduced to the organization's cultural climate and its undocumented but very real structure of social diplomacy (internal politics). That is, stated more succinctly, organizations lack a process of introducing the executive to "the way we do things around here."

Whenever an executive fails to gain traction and find a place in an organization, the executive search consultant who did the recruiting makes an easy scapegoat, regardless of how well the courtship process went, because of the myth that behind every failed executive is a failed executive search process. The executive who failed also blames the search process.

Those in the business of senior leadership recruiting—as part of the employer organization's executive staffing team or from an executive search firm—are judged partly on their recruiting performance and equally on whether the leaders they recruit into the organization excel from the start or crash and burn. Thus they have a serious vested interest in executive onboarding because failure to integrate new leaders successfully often leads to a resignation or an awkward and costly firing—and inevitably comes back to haunt the recruiter. Executive-level recruiters look much better in the eyes of their clients—be they line managers, CEOs, directors, or others—if they advocate for and contribute to the executive integration process so that their recruits onboard effectively and don't get tossed out as a result of avoidable missteps.

Whenever an executive fails to gain traction, the executive search consultant makes an easy scapegoat.

James P. Mooney, a senior vice president and senior consultant with Farr Associates, says the executive search consultant can seek to accomplish several objectives in the onboarding process. First, he argues, the search consultant can "raise the importance level of onboarding in the eyes of both the hiring executive and the placed executive—a difficult task in that the search consultant is also trying to convince the client how perfectly the candidate fits their requirements!" But if the need is not established during the recruitment process, Mooney says, "it's pretty hard to do it afterwards."

Second, the search consultant can "identify the players who are key to the placed executive's success, and coordinate with the onboarding consultant on involvement of those players." Very often, Mooney explains, the hiring executive has a search to complete, and once it's done, that person is not directly connected with or involved in the placed executive's success or failure. "The onboarding consultant needs all the help he or she can get to be able through coaching to direct the placed executive's efforts at the key relationships."

Third, Mooney says, the executive recruiter can recognize "the value of the process in making the placement stick and in developing with the client a reputation for solid placements."

AVOIDING EXECUTIVE-LEVEL ORGAN REJECTION

Think of onboarding as a twenty-first-century form of executive employee orientation to the people, projects, priorities, and cultural identity and nuance that define the rules of engagement and the workplace environment for an organization and for a particular role. But also think of onboarding as an essential step to avoid executive-level organ rejection. That's because executives have a major impact on so many other parts of the business and the organizational culture, much in the same way the vital organs feed, nourish, and sustain multiple parts of the human body. The cultural ripple effect—let alone the huge cost-related side effects—of a bad executive hire can be as catastrophic and irreversible for the hiring organization as the loss of a vital organ can be for an otherwise healthy person—leading to debilitation, paralysis, or even doom.

Onboarding would certainly have helped a lot of executives who, because of their own stumble out of the blocks or some unfortunate twist of circumstances beyond their control, were in trouble right from the start. It might have given them just the kind of insider information they needed to see how they were being perceived before it was too late, and it might have come at just the right time to develop an effective action plan.

Think of onboarding as an essential step to avoid executive-level organ rejection.

But all too often, without the support of an effective onboarding program, new executives don't even realize they are in trouble or out of step with their boss, peers, or board until the moment they get fired. Some fail to realize that they've been put under the organization's microscope, and that everything they say and do—and fail to say and do—is constantly being interpreted and misinterpreted by others interested in gauging their tone and their approach to making things happen.

There's a honeymoon stage to every senior management job, but given the intense external pressures that are mounting on executive and organizational performance these days, the term of that grace period is undoubtedly shrinking. An early misstep or ungraceful entry into a new environment may amount to a real missed opportunity.

And given the escalation of senior management pay, top executives may have precious little time to prove they're worth what their new employers paid to recruit or promote them into the hot seat. "Companies have an increasing need for high-performance executives, but they are given only a limited amount of time in which to produce results. It used to be two or three years. Now we're seeing that shrink to as little as twelve to eigh-teen months," says Pearl Meyer, cofounder and senior managing director of Steven Hall & Partners, an independent executive compensation and governance consulting firm based in New York.

Meyer, who led an executive search practice before embarking on a career that has made her one of America's most experienced and widely admired executive pay consultants, says this new "short fuse on providing results" has made the work of top executive recruiters much more difficult because of the risk senior corporate officers perceive in leaving their current position, where they have established a proven record of success. "A real chill sets in when they consider the challenge and question whether the 'honeymoon' period will permit them enough time to get the job done," Meyer says.

One question to convey the urgency of the particular leadership need and get newly recruited or promoted executives thinking about their entry into the new environment and the expected tempo of their decision making is this: What exactly are you going to do your first day on the job?

COMMITMENT FOR A WIN-WIN SITUATION

Employer organizations that understand the executive employment life cycle—from recruitment and selection through development and retention—understand that attracting and hiring the right person is only the beginning, and that onboarding buys the executive time to lay the groundwork for a long-term contribution to performance.

Organizations even might justifiably expect bigger, better, and faster results when they care to invest some resources to help get a new executive into the organizational flow and feeling good about making a good start toward accomplishing the objectives of the position. That's essential, because decisions made by the new leader in the first few weeks—perhaps even in the first few days—on the job can have a lasting impact.

"Leadership roles are increasingly of the 'hit the ground running' variety," says Laurence J. Stybel, a founding partner of Board Options, Inc., and Stybel Peabody Lincolnshire, a Boston-area consultancy that specializes in managing leadership change. "In the interview, the hiring authorities ask, 'Can you hit the ground running?' The candidate says, 'Of course I can hit the ground running, and here are some examples of what I have done.'"

But invariably, Stybel contends, that kind of expectation setting moves new leaders toward doing what worked well the last time they had to hit the ground running. "And that may or may not apply well in this specific situation," he explains. "Leadership errors made in the first one hundred days are far more consequential than similar errors made [during] the second year of a leadership role."

Stybel describes three kinds of leadership mandates: *continuity,* which calls for business as usual, especially in the case of an interim leader being named until a search for an external successor can be completed; *good to great,* which borrows on the best-selling book's prescription for elevating corporate performance; and *turnaround,* which demands drastic change and leaves no process, job, or strategy out of bounds.

Employer organizations, Stybel adds, also need to understand that any leadership integration program that is "opt-in" will probably only result in the new leader saying, "I can save you money right away. I told you I had a black belt in hitting the ground running. I don't need the service." It's far better for an executive search consultant, the hiring manager, or a senior HR executive to maintain that the onboarding program—in whatever form—is an organizational expectation that the executive can't simply choose to avoid. Setting the expectation up front helps the employer clearly communicate its commitment to a win-win situation.

Leadership errors made in the first one hundred days are far more consequential than similar errors made [during] the second year.

Part of setting the expectation for any leadership post, Stybel notes, lies in the employer's ability to enunciate exactly what is expected of the individual executive. "There is an inherent conflict between the job description as an accurate descriptor of a job and a job description as advancing the corporate image in the marketplace," he says. "The result of this conflict is that leadership job descriptions are often written as 'good to great' leadership mandates. The interviews are conducted on this basis and the selection is conducted on this basis."

A potential problem may arise, Stybel suggests, when the leader starts the job (and the transaction-oriented recruiter has left the scene for a new search) and "finds out that there are two mandates: an expressed one and a stealth one."

Stybel believes newly hired and newly promoted leaders and their employers should ask three questions:[4]

- "What needs to be changed within the next 12 months?"
- "What needs to be honored or kept within the next 12 months?"
- "What must be avoided at all costs?"

PUTTING ONBOARDING INTO PRACTICE

It has always been essential to get the right executive leaders into the right roles. Today, given the unprecedented turnover in the corporate management ranks, it is important to support new leaders during their transition periods—particularly in the most complex situations and organizations. Quite simply, new executives are under pressure to perform from day one, if not before then.

Over the course of his twenty-year career, Kevin Roche has held senior HR positions with Raytheon Corporation, Bristol-Myers Squibb Company, Keane, Student Advantage, and Reebok International. In each of those roles, he's gained important perspectives about corporate best practices in executive onboarding. Roche recalls that during the late 1990s, the pressure for new executive leaders to perform was particularly intense, especially in the start-up and dot-com business environment. "They expected these significant leaders to perform right out of the gates and they expected those leaders literally to transform themselves and the business overnight," and that was unrealistic, Roche says.

Yet while the immediate demands on many start-up company leaders were rolled back after the dot-com economy caved in, the expectations on those in new leadership roles in all companies have been steadily rebuilding ever since.

Roche recalls one instance in which a CEO approached the corporation's new president only nine days into his role and asked, "What have you done for me?" The CEO, Roche says, "expected rock star results. It was unbelievable, and the president was flabbergasted. The president responded only by saying, 'I don't even know where the men's room is yet.' And frankly, that said a lot more about the CEO than it did the new president!"

The worst-case situation, Roche says, is when an organization rejects the new leader. That can involve subtleties like excluding the person from meetings and memos. "That's when it becomes a fait accompli for the new leader," he says.

Roche recalls another corporate experience that pushed his employer to take onboarding seriously. "We had a constant churn at the leadership level, and that naturally led us to . . . question . . . what we were really getting as a return on our investment. We saw a string of executives either crash and burn or we'd swap them out, from the president to the divisional levels of leadership," he recalls. Ultimately, the company got the message.

"We've spent a lot of time and effort to bring this talent into the organization and what better way to optimize that talent than to support it through onboarding?" Roche says. "Their success is our success, and at the end of the day, success for the individual is about the execution of the strategy."

Sometimes, Roche says, an executive will walk in with a plan, but it really needs to be something that HR, the executive, the person the executive reports to, his or her mentor, and—as is usually the case in larger organizations—someone from the talent management function all build some consensus around. "It's a variety of people who need to be involved," he says.

The mentoring and coaching that can be provided by a high-performing executive who already knows the cultural and political lay of the land is indispensable for the new leader. In some leading organizations, Roche says, "New executives are paired up with an executive who's been around a while . . . and they're also expected to produce a formal, written hundred-day plan."

Further, Roche adds, "I think it's always great to see an executive who has a plan as well as the flexibility to adapt the plan to the current situation and this group of plan builders, as opposed to simply trying to advance a plan that worked for them in the past."

He says an executive's hundred-day onboarding plan should address short-term goals related to business continuity, strategy, organizational structure, and execution against that strategy. "It's really about the structure, roles, organizational plans, and an assessment of the talent around them," he adds. "They need to simultaneously factor in any changes they may want to make and they need to understand the systems, processes, governance structure, committees, and any baseline training they may require."

Most important, he points out, "They need to establish key relationships. One person can't run a company, so it's all about galvanizing the resources to drive the kind of change they want to drive."

One onboarding best practice is to engage new executives and their direct reports in a facilitated discussion that focuses on tough questions about expectations, perceptions, and team alignment to business strategy roughly a hundred days into their tenure. In this kind of session, the team gathers and answers questions such as What does the new leader need to know about the team? and What would you like to see the leader do with the team?

After garnering input about how the leader is being perceived, how his or her communication style fits with team expectations, and other cultural observations, the facilitator then meets privately with the executive for a debriefing on the team session and a start at fashioning appropriate responses. The team, the facilitator, and the new leader then come together to discuss their observations.

"It culminates in the leader and the team making a commitment and agreeing on how they're going to work together moving forward," Roche says, adding that it usually produces great results.

ONBOARDING TO ACCELERATE LEADERSHIP IMPACT

George Bradt, founder of the New York–based executive onboarding and transition acceleration firm PrimeGenesis, is the author of *The*

New Leader's 100-Day Action Plan (Wiley, 2006), a practical guidebook for executives and those who hire them about navigating the potentially treacherous waters of an executive-level transition. Bradt points out that professional golfers have both coaches and caddies, and new executives need the same kinds of help.

Coaches serve as behind-the-scenes advisers between tournaments. "Caddies . . . do provide advice and counsel," Bradt says, "but their real value is in their tangible contributions on the field of play. They accelerate progress through what they do as well as what they say. In the most complex transitions, that extra leverage can make all the difference."

Today, regardless of the intensity of the challenges for new leaders, Bradt says, all parties involved—recruiter, organization, and new leader—should see the transition process as having two steps: invest to get the right leaders into the right roles, and then provide appropriate support to them during their transitions.

Providing Support

As we have seen, executive recruiters own the first step in the transition process. They can also assist in the second step by making sure the organization has the right mentor, transition coach, and performance feedback mechanism in place to support the new executive at work.

Some best practices related to executive onboarding, Bradt says, should be on the radar screen of both executive-level recruiters and talent management executives:

- Helping a newly hired or recently promoted executives identify key stakeholders in the organization at some point before the official start date
- Mapping out how new executives will spend time toward achieving goals on the first day, in the first few weeks, and in the first hundred days on the job. Identifying early wins is critical.

- Giving new executives the leeway to mobilize their team. That means
  - Supporting people who are in the right role and performing well
  - Moving people who are in the wrong role and performing poorly
  - Investing in people who are in the right role but not performing well
  - Shifting into new roles any people who are performing well but in the wrong role
- Adjusting to inevitable surprises. That means taking stock of when something beyond a new executive's control is major and enduring, which should force a new look at leadership strategy; or understanding that the change is just a temporary obstacle, which may call for revising the tactical approach but maintaining the basic strategy.

Bradt believes successful executive onboarding is all about helping new executives make the biggest impact with the most important stakeholders, build trust and loyalty, and manage communications inside and outside the organization.

Besides the kind of multi-appraiser performance assessment surveys that provide meaningful institutional lessons for the executive, a growing number of tools and resources can support new leaders with their transitions, as depicted in Table 3. Bradt says the more complex the situation and orientation and the more urgent the transition, the more intensive the support should be. *Internal mentoring* is the least intensive, and is appropriate when all the new leader needs is on-the-job knowledge sharing. Next in line is *transition coaching,* where behind-the-scenes leadership development is useful. And in the most complex situations, hands-on, operationally experienced *transition acceleration* merits consideration.

Transition accelerators work with new leaders and their teams across what Bradt describes as the "three stages of onboarding":

TABLE 3 **One Onboarding Consultant's Support Programs**

Program Type	**Internal Mentoring** Generally informal	**Transition Coaching** Personal advice and counsel for *leader*	**Transition Acceleration** Experience-based help for *team* across key tasks
Objective	Knowledge sharing	Leadership development	Jump-start team performance
Environment	On the job	Behind the scenes	In the room, with the team
Assistance provided	• Network access • Moral support • Communication	• Advice and counsel • Scenario planning • Role-play for practice	• Drive better results faster • Hands-on work on strategy, people, and culture
Authority	Company knowledge	Process skills	Operational experience
Situation	Stable	Mixed	Unsettled
Orientation	Promoted in place	"Internal" transfer	New to company/ culture
Urgency	Time to learn	Balanced	Acute need to act

Source: Adapted from and used with permission of PrimeGenesis.

- **Preboarding:** Work with the new leader to create an onboarding plan and to build relationships with key stakeholders in the new organization even before day one.
- **Day one:** Help the new leader take charge of those critical initial impressions.
- **First hundred days:** Work with the new leader to accelerate the development of a high-performing team through workshops, milestone management processes, identification and delivery of

early wins, timely reassignment of team roles as necessary, and communication plans.

Tracking the Results

So what is the organizational impact of effective executive onboarding?

"It certainly creates some velocity. It accelerates the speed at which leaders build relationships and mesh with the culture, and they can learn more quickly," says Kevin Roche, the longtime corporate HR executive. "I think the performance is better and you see the results of that better performance much more quickly," he adds. "And the better integrated the leader, based on my experience, the longer they stay in the organization because they've built credibility, they've developed relationships and made a good start."

The positive outcomes generated through senior management onboarding and integration programs are multiplying. And search consultants are just beginning to track how onboarding extends the tenure and aids the retention of executives they recruit.

ARAMARK, a global leader in food and facility management services, found that the turnover rate for external hires in its executive ranks was over 25 percent. The expense created by a series of recruitment cycles was mounting, not to mention the loss in productivity while a stream of senior managers worked their way through the system. An initial survey of the organization by executive and organization development firm RHR International indicated that the culture of the company was challenging for outsiders.

In an industry marked by intense competition for the best talent, Bristol-Myers Squibb found it was retaining only 40 percent of its outside executive hires. The company's approach to assessment lacked rigor and its integration process was minimal and inconsistent. When the company did find and hire a candidate who was ideal for its business, it had no means to ensure the newcomer's success.

New onboarding programs at ARAMARK and Bristol-Myers Squibb helped both companies accelerate new executives' integration, educate employees about the process, and provide a feedback link between the new executive and the organization.

Bristol-Myers Squibb institutionalized a process through which the same executive and organization development firm assesses a hundred senior-level candidates annually in North America, Europe, and Asia, and hires and integrates thirty to forty executives. The retention rate for outside hires in the executive ranks has climbed to near 90 percent.

At ARAMARK, dozens of executives have participated in the program to date, with a positive impact on retention rates. The program is a significant organizational change initiative, and many managers and HR personnel now have a better understanding of the key success factors and derailers for new hires.

What's more, communication and dialogue around integration have increased. Warning signs of retention risks are being highlighted and managed more quickly than in the past. Take, for example, the case of a CEO who credited onboarding with breaking a logjam in his communications and working relationship with the board of directors. Prior to the appraisal of his performance and the feedback sessions with an onboarding consultant, the executive operated "in isolation, never 100 percent clear about how they wanted him to interface with them, involve them in decisions, draw on their experience," says Farr Associates' James P. Mooney. "The assessment data gave him a 'point of entry,'" he adds, "to improve those relationships, and the coaching by our consultant provided the tactical advice he needed to make the most of it."

The chief operating officer of a large medical center says the onboarding program he participated in helped him understand the impact of his management style. "The coaching helped me identify reasons I was seen as ineffective in some areas."

Mooney says the proof is in the pudding, and employers, executives, and search consultants can expect results like these from a corporate investment in onboarding:

- Quicker integration of the executive into the employer's culture
- Lower incidence of culture-shift shock

- Less time wasted in false starts, and smaller withdrawals from emotional bank accounts
- More rapid and energetic alignment with the change initiative that usually accompanies the placement

Looking ahead, HR executive Kevin Roche believes more executives—whether recruited externally or promoted from within—will ask for onboarding support to prevent an early misstep from taking a huge toll on their career.

Evidence is mounting that effective executive onboarding significantly improves the durability of executive hires and accelerates their "time to contribution," both critical measures of individual and organizational success in a global economy that demands speed, performance, and continual improvement.

The more softly and effectively executives land in a new leadership post, the more quickly they gain momentum, build rapport, and gain confidence. That moves them closer to achieving objectives and establishing their own lasting identity in the organization.

8

PARTNERS IN LEADERSHIP RECRUITING

The successful partnering between client and search firm is a two-sided arrangement that requires substantial measures of trust, chemistry and professional respect.

PETER BENNETT[1]

Many multinational and emerging companies have only recently launched initiatives to develop crisis succession plans, "high-potential" employee development programs, management performance appraisals, and talent pipeline investment. Many others haven't even started or can't see that now is the time to invest in their leadership future. Worse yet, many companies continue to engage a variety of search consultants without really understanding the kinds of results they should expect—and commit to enabling—and how the terms of engagement with informed outsiders preordain those results.

Both the corporate and search firm parties to the leadership succession challenge have long struggled to measure the effectiveness of their executive-level recruiting. "Quality of hire" is emerging as one important although extremely variable measure of that impact.

It hasn't helped that HR executives and executive search consultants often run afoul of each other. Part of the long-standing dysfunction of corporate management succession and leadership recruiting is that these two key facilitating agents of the senior management hiring process frequently fail to work as effective partners in solving strategic business challenges. Instead, the two groups usually maintain an uneasy coexistence. Sometimes they achieve partnership, cooperation, and respect, but sometimes the relationship is characterized more by conflict, marginalization, enmity, boundary clashes, and mutual disrespect. The inconsistent, haphazard, adversarial, confused, and often ineffectual nature of the most unhealthy of those relationships has impaired corporate performance and impeded the search for executive leadership advantage.

The genesis of these sometimes-calamitous relations among talent specialists inside and outside the organization is found in the business cycle itself and the way it invariably shifts control of the employment proposition from the organization to the desired management candidate and back to the employer. What results is something of a power struggle, or what one former corporate staffing officer once described, rather diplomatically, as "an interesting push-pull" that leaves the corporation and its preferred executive search consultants with equal responsibility for failed executive management recruiting.

When business is booming, employers eager to grow their operations turn to executive search consultants to deliver the requisite management talent to get the job done. Exceptionally qualified executives then find themselves in the driver's seat, and search consultants are uniquely positioned to facilitate the courtship process. But recruiters sometimes exploit and oversell their reach, access, and connections to candidates and their own ability to tackle more work. Or at least that is how they are perceived by HR leaders inside the client company.

Anytime search consultants' performance reveals itself (or is seen by others) to be inconsistent or their motives for taking on a new search assignment seem less than admirable, HR executives take note, including those who have, over time, moved from the "Personnel

Department" to "Staffing" to "Talent Acquisition" without actually changing jobs. And they exact their own form of organizational retribution when corporate earnings shrink, management recruiting becomes more selective, and the economic pendulum swings in favor of employers and leaves many executive recruiters scrounging for new business.

Likewise, when HR policies begin to commoditize the delivery of executive search consulting and put the squeeze on engagement fees, search consultants tend to put their resources behind more valuable client relationships. And the search consultants likewise hold a grudge.

All parties are responsible for the power struggles that impair executive recruiting effectiveness, and all must realize that they have vested interests in working collaboratively to achieve the leadership objectives of the organization they together serve. Executive recruiters, HR or talent acquisition executives, and the line executives they both assist need to reassess how they do business with one another and find common ground so they can maximize their joint efforts to deliver results through superior quality of management.

The most senior management leaders, including the CEO, CFO, COO, and general counsel, "must know how and when to mediate, to conciliate, to negotiate" in their dealings with their own HR agents and executive search consultants, all of whom have a vested interest in establishing or elevating the quality of the organization's leadership.[2] The biggest challenge to organizational stability and growth is filling the senior management succession pipeline, and rising to that unprecedented challenge will require an equally unprecedented fusion of resources, perspectives, and objectives between HR leaders and executive search consultants.

HR FROM THE EXECUTIVE SEARCH CONSULTANT'S POINT OF VIEW

To realize that union of interests, search consultants may have to shift some of their long-standing views about the value of working purposefully with a client organization's HR and executive staffing or talent acquisition and talent management liaisons. At present, legions of executive search consultants believe they are far more attuned than HR, which administers the people side of the business, to the issues (especially external market forces) that are pressuring the organization to shift its priorities and investment in business planning. They also widely believe that their proximity to senior corporate leaders and their market intelligence about just who may be recruitable put them in a better position to understand the company's executive leadership needs than most HR practitioners, who, they believe, are far less entrepreneurial and business savvy. The few in-house exceptions that executive recruiters regard as having a handle on their own business are almost uniformly referred to as "strategic HR leaders."

The contempt that some search consultants harbor for corporate HR officers isn't far removed from the way HR is sometimes maligned and described as frustratingly ineffectual and nonstrategic by other units within the same company.

Leading companies do include their top HR people in the strategy-setting process, and engage with them and solicit their input as that strategy is communicated to the people who must deliver results that support it. But in recent years, HR has come under attack from virtually all sides, and the media—from television to print to the blogosphere—haven't missed the chance to pile on. Consider the front cover of the August 2005 issue of *Fast Company,* which led with this headline and teaser: "Why We Hate HR: Human Resources strangles us with rules, cuts our benefits and blocks constructive change. It has to do better."

Some search consultants believe that corporate staffing units are repositories for former executive recruiters who couldn't hack it with search consulting firms or for career "HR-ists" who just don't measure up to more entrepreneurial, strategic challenges. "Not a lot of people in life set out to become an HR executive," says a distinguished retired search consultant. But the same, it must be noted, applies equally to the field of executive search consulting.

Many executive search consultants make no effort to disguise their distaste for working directly with HR, as they prefer to parachute into strategic conversations about business challenges. That is, they go over the heads of HR officers and develop dialogue with the C-suite and with executives on the front lines of the business.

It is true that within many organizations HR is still not recognized as a strategic partner in the success of the enterprise. Search consultants want to work with the most strategic people and elements of their client companies. Perhaps the search business shouldn't be blamed entirely for wanting to avoid direct collaboration or association with the HR function, but as HR becomes more strategic, more search consultants may gravitate toward it.

Some search consultants complain that they're forced to spend a lot of time educating clients and potential clients about the work they do, or that HR tends to regard the product of the search solely as a candidate, instead of seeing the much broader implications of the candidate's vision, leadership, and networks.

"They're either your best friend or your worst enemy," says one search consultant, who adds, "You're constantly in conflict with HR, because you're doing a job they couldn't do themselves." Says another: "There is a surprising number of unsophisticated buyers, even in pretty large, well-known companies." Still another chimes in: "While they use us, most of them don't understand us."

HR needs to work internally to lubricate the search process by facilitating effective and timely decisions that affect the course of the search assignment and by rallying internal support for exemplary candidates who may not be on the market for long.

One searcher expresses concern that hiring organizations don't always treat short-listed candidates with courtesy, professionalism, and grace. "It's a big mistake not to treat everyone respectfully," he says, because "It's a small [world] we live in." But the truth is that search consultants are at least equally guilty of the same lapses in professional courtesy, and that their clashes with HR are often prompted by disputes and miscommunications whose genesis lies elsewhere in the hiring organization.

So under what conditions does a search consultant like to work with its client hiring organization and its agents in the executive search process? Here is one consultant's uniquely expressive and candid exploration of the search consultant's client wish list and pet peeves.

We like clients who:

- See the recruitment of senior executives as a powerful competitive weapon; get that recruited candidates are not applicants and that interview experience will define their ongoing interest; inject charm and finesse into the courtship process
- Regard us as a trusted advisor or personal shopper, not a vendor; recognize that we are not trying to "get away" with anything or sneak a slapshot past the goalie; allow us to own responsibility for candidate quality and flow; don't second-guess us (although they may certainly push back ad hoc)
- Rely on *our* perceptions and instincts about people, specifically with regard to likely success within each client culture; know that we didn't just start doing this last week
- Trust the accuracy of *their* perceptions and instincts about people and can clearly articulate those data points to us, calibrating and modifying in collaboration with ours
- Are willing to be open and honest with us about the shortcomings or failures of their current executive teams and functions
- Actively participate with us in raising the "talent bar" for their organization; understand that their objectives and ours are identical; care about the long-term relationship with us
- Respond quickly to our suggestions and coaching; appreciate that timing is everything in recruitment; demonstrate a sense of urgency (not desperation)
- Think in terms of value rather than cost

Conversely, we dislike clients who:

- Imagine they're entitled to recruit and hire anyone they might be able to describe; don't have a realistic "body image" in terms of whom they might legitimately attract
- Think and act like bureaucrats; bury us in process, protocol, and superfluous communications; can't schedule effectively; don't see interviews as a priority
- Have little or no experience working with retained search firms; can't keep track of who's at bat, who's on base, and what the score is; don't have a sense of rhythm or timing; imagine that they are expert at candidate assessment and evaluation; fail to understand the importance of timely, substantive feedback on candidates
- Don't have at least a couple of exceedingly talented executives on board already (around whom we can focus and spin our recruitment efforts)
- Mistake organizational pathology for "culture"; harbor and empower clueless executives who are considered vital for inscrutable reasons; punish independence, frankness, and ruthless self-evaluation (both internally and in relation to outside entities such as us)
- Believe that their execution problems are anecdotal, cosmetic, or situational rather than systemic; enjoy scapegoating consultants who try to fix their problems
- Can't see themselves as others perceive them (so important I mention it twice); prefer to work with search firms who suck up; fail to appreciate our genius and heroic efforts on their behalf
- Don't pay on time; change the project deliverables and expect no additional fees; fail to sing our praises to anyone who will listen

---

Source: Mark Jaffe, President, Wyatt & Jaffe

EXECUTIVE SEARCH CONSULTANTS FROM THE HR PERSPECTIVE

Few within the HR world would argue with the assertion that the people side of business needs to be more strategic, more flexible, and more fluid to address the talent needs that arise from the emergence, transformation, and realignment of corporate management roles. "More and more companies are asking their Human Resources departments, 'How can you help us secure our competitive advantage?'" according to M. Bernadette Patton, president and CEO of the Human Resource Management Association of Chicago (HRMAC).[3] With more than six hundred member companies, HRMAC is the oldest independent regional corporate membership association in the United States.

"In the old days, we were more likely to focus on due dates for benefits enrollment or hear questions like, 'Did the paychecks get out on time?'" Patton recalls. "HR departments [now] have to demonstrate a deeper strategic value for a company."

Much in the same way search consultants downgrade HR for what it can't see and can't deliver, or hold that function accountable for broader organizational dysfunction, many HR professionals resent executive search consultants for what they promise but fail to achieve, for their access to senior management, and for the arrogance, greed, self-absorption, and pretentiousness that more than a few recruiters radiate.

Frustration with search consultants runs high among some in the HR function, but part of that angst can be explained, says one longtime corporate HR executive, in that "Most HR people simply don't understand executive search."

The frustration also has other causes, however. One senior vice president of human resources who bases her views on her own experience says she's done with "paying and getting nothing" from executive search consultants, some of whom excel at selling the business but fall down when it comes to actually executing it, and extremely few of whom would even consider offering a refund to a dissatisfied client. The former director of executive recruiting with a large corporation adds of her experience with search consultants: "There really is very little to no value add. There is no innovation. They're going back to the practices that worked for them fifteen years ago."

Others describe executive search consultants as akin to used car sales agents, or worse. One retired search consultant admits: "Search firms are overpopulated by highly aggressive, ambitious, fast-talking, fast-walking warriors with a book-and-bill mentality instead of [people focused on] taking the time to do things right."

Jacques P. "Jay" Andre Jr., who leads executive hiring for global management consulting firm Booz Allen Hamilton, worked for almost seven years in executive search consulting before he joined the firm to coordinate internal and external assignments to recruit vice presidents and principals, its two most senior management levels. Today, he leads the firm's team of in-house talent researchers and recruiters and is also responsible for managing the firm's relationships with executive search consultants.

"I know some of my compatriots in positions like mine have a resentment or dislike for [search consultants]," he says. "I don't . . . they're very useful. There are certain elements that are hyperaggressive, sales-focused, and more interested in bagging the search sale than recruiting the executive. You've just got to watch out for these [people] through experience and networking."

Andre and the firm choose to work with executive search consultants who continually affirm Booz Allen Hamilton's engagement decision. "I think world-class executive search consulting is when you're working with someone who is really engaged, has taken the effort to understand your needs and your issues, and is not just there to sell their firm but to actively listen."

But it's important for HR leaders and anyone else who engages an executive search consultant to understand that, as Andre says, "A successful search doesn't necessarily mean you got a hire." From his experience, 20 percent to 30 percent of search assignments don't end in an executive's hiring. This outcome occurs for a variety of reasons, such as the hiring organization's decision to

A successful search doesn't necessarily mean you got a hire.

cancel a search after it's already launched or a delay in decision making that lets a top candidate get away.

While he goes into every search assignment expecting to hire an exceptional leader, Andre says the true value Booz Allen Hamilton gets from the search consulting engagement lies in answers to questions such as these:

- Was the process well managed and does it instruct our future engagements?
- Did the assignment give us a new read on the markets we serve?
- Have we nonetheless met and opened the lines of communication with some outstanding leaders from other organizations?

Of course, the best executive search consulting delivers positive results on all those metrics and also delivers an outstanding executive who makes a valuable short-term and long-term contribution to the hiring organization's success. "The cherry on top is you got a great executive," Andre says.

But acquiring a highly qualified leader for a senior management role doesn't always guarantee that the hiring company will come back to the same executive search consultant for the next assignment. Sometimes the firm chooses not to engage a consultant who successfully recruited a new executive, and other times it engages a firm that may have delivered exceptional market insight during the course of a search that didn't end with an executive's hiring. Of the latter circumstance, Andre says, "That's probably the best endorsement a search firm can get."

Andre says he's learned a lot from having made the transition from outside search consultant to corporate leadership recruiter. "I've gotten a new respect [for HR's role], having gone over to the corporate side," he says. One of those lessons, and one he probably didn't fully appreciate when he was employed by an executive search consulting firm, Andre says, was this: "It's almost always a mistake to do an end run around a [corporate] recruiting or HR person who's been put in the position of middleman" between the external search consultant and a corporate line manager with a significant management talent need.

Given the increasing complexity of executive employment agreements, internal executive recruiters and HR leaders can lend considerable experience and guidance. Their insight reflects corporate concern for how the new executive is screened and ultimately onboarded, and for regulatory issues, especially in sectors such as government. "There are valid reasons for HR and recruitment to be involved in the [external] search process," Andre notes, adding that search consultants who would rather avoid HR "don't understand the power [of] an HR person whose nose is out of joint to slow up and grind the search to a stop. They can either gum up the works or they can be a powerful, positive influencer and facilitator of the external search process."

While Jay Andre has learned a lot about the challenges of leadership recruiting, having made the transition from executive search consultant, his father, Jacques P. "Jac" Andre, who retired after nearly forty years as an executive search consultant, knows exactly what it's like to go the other way. The elder Andre recalls that in 1965 he was "searched out" of P. Ballantine & Sons, then one of the largest brewers in the United States, by an executive recruiter who gave him his first job in executive search with Ernst & Ernst (now Ernst & Young) in New York.

"I had to learn the search business and the method of how to identify candidates and how to approach them. I improved my interview skills," he says, "and I saw it as a job that combined personnel (human resources) and sales, because you couldn't do a search without first selling it."

Jac Andre took an immediate liking to executive search because "my bosses were my clients" and "if I kept clients happy, brought in revenue, and did quality work, all [my search firm] wanted to do was help me be better." That was unlike the challenge he faced as an HR executive: "Dealing with corporate politics and managing through a bureaucracy to get things accomplished." Successful partnering between search consultant and HR executive, he says, requires that the search consultant learn how to sell business but also how to evaluate leadership candidates' fit for a particular management opportunity.

Another particularly astute facilitator, consumer, and observer of the HR-search firm engagement process is Lucien Alziari, who worked for British Rail and Mars U.K. Ltd. before assuming senior HR leadership positions with regional units and, ultimately, the corporate division of PepsiCo and later Avon Products as senior vice president of human resources. Alziari offered some timeless advice some years ago during a presentation to a conference of the International Association for Corporate and Professional Recruitment (see Table 4).

Part of the reason there is little love lost between HR officers and executive search consultants is the way executive recruiting, by its nature, tends to skew the kind of traditional and overall cost-per-hire metrics that have been a hallmark of old-school HR. Every employer must draw the line between strategic recruiting—where the need for external management talent requires a commensurate investment—and recruiting farther down the organizational chart, where cost-per-hire is a better gauge of recruiting effectiveness because of the sheer volume of new hires (though even there it can't be the only gauge of effectiveness).

Given the price of going outside at the executive level, it's no wonder that some HR officers would use the inconsistency of executive search firms as justification for altering the traditional rules of engagement or relegating search assignments to recruiting vendors who qualify as lowest bidder or bring a pay-for-results approach to their billing.

Former executive search consultant Rick Helliwell, vice president of recruitment in the HR unit of Dubai-based Emirates Airline and Group, says that the realities of competing for top executives' attention and reaching them through executive search consultants' networks is critical to sustaining the organization's leadership edge.

"Any large organization which is expanding will have to at some point look externally to hire in senior candidates, and it is well accepted that many of the top senior executives do not read job boards or scour newspapers or magazines unless actively on the market. They're just

TABLE 4 How HR Can Contribute to Management Succession Success: Ten Key Lessons from the Course of an Executive Search Assignment

1. HR says to the executive search consultant: *"Find me a great marketer."*

This may be more specific than the typical job specification or mandate provided by HR.

HR Takeaway: Know the business, be clear on the need, define success.

2. Line executive to the search consultant: *"Find me a great marketer in 30 days."*

Start with a clear project plan, align internal executives on the plan, ensure regular (fact- or milestone-based) updates, hold the search consultant to the timeline, and help maintain the momentum of the search by facilitating internal scheduling of interviews with search consultant and most promising candidates.

HR Takeaway: Own the process from start to finish.

3. Search consultant to HR executive: *"Do you have any feedback on those candidate profiles I sent you ten days ago?"*

The search consultant needs HR to help calibrate the suitability of candidates and keep the process moving.

HR Takeaway: Provide timely feedback on candidate slates.

4. Search consultant to HR executive: *"I support your diversity initiative...I just can't find a diverse candidate at that level."*

Hold executive search consultants to their promise. If they have agreed to deliver a diverse slate, remind them that the job isn't done unless they do.

HR Takeaway: Stay focused on job spec, hold consultants accountable.

5. Very senior line executive to HR executive: *"If that's the best search firm X can do, we've got real problems."*

Choose the first candidate(s) who'll be interviewed internally very carefully, because these interactions help set expectations about the tempo and direction of the process. Don't rush the process by introducing less-than-stellar candidates.

HR Takeaway: Remember that perceptions about initial candidate(s) will shape the outcome.

TABLE 9 CONT'D

6. HR executive to search consultant: *"We didn't like him/her. It's not a fit."*

Give the search consultant precise and actionable feedback on the perceived quality of candidates introduced in the search process.

HR Takeaway: Give feedback that will help refine the search.

7. HR executive to the search consultant: *"We loved him/her. Keep him/her warm."*

Take personal ownership of the top candidates who emerge from the interviewing process. Begin to build a personal relationship with them.

HR Takeaway: Shift ownership of the assignment from searcher to HR.

8. Line executive to HR executive: *"We can't afford to wait any longer."*

Move the pace of the search to "hurry-up offense" and work with the search consultant to accelerate the introduction of any final top-notch candidates.

HR Takeaway: Give line executive someone he or she can get excited about.

9. HR executive to HR executive: *"I really liked him/her. When can he/she start?"*

The pressure to seal the deal begins to intensify, yet it's important to avoid nasty surprises that upset the process. Use the search consultant to test ideas, frame the opportunity, and reinforce key messages. Make a "scoping offer" of employment revealing what is negotiable and what is not to move the negotiations forward.

HR Takeaway: Let the search consultant find the mutual commitment.

10. HR executive to anyone who'll listen: *"Can you really have too much talent?"*

The search now successfully completed, the HR executive appreciates that the search for exceptional talent requires his or her involvement, the commitment of senior/line management and the outside perspective that an executive search consultant brings.

HR Takeaway: Everyone has to know and commit to his or her role in the executive search process.

Source: Quoted and adapted from Lucien Alziari, "The Successful Search: What Goes on Inside the Corporation," presentation to the IACPR, New York, October 19, 2003.

too busy," Helliwell says. "The need for a trusted, well-respected, and credible 'search partner' with global networks is clearly very important," he adds. "When it comes to your business's leadership [and] where you will get the highest ROI for the right investment (selection) decision, you don't want to take risks. You need to take time to ensure the right search partner is selected and be prepared to make tough decisions."

Many HR professionals view executive recruiters as transaction specialists and nothing more. Search consultants as strategic business partners? To some strategic HR executives like Helliwell, yes, indeed. To many others, however, fat chance—they simply haven't earned the distinction. Of the transaction-oriented, one search consultant says: "They'll be happy with the money they saved but not necessarily happy with the caliber of executive hires they made."

When it comes to your business's leadership . . . you don't want to take risks. You need to take time to ensure the right search partner is selected and be prepared to make tough decisions.

TOWARD TRUE PARTNERSHIP

It's clear that an increasing number of hiring companies are reevaluating or rebalancing the build-or-buy emphasis in their leadership recruiting. Employers are clearly desirous of more intimate relationships with their chosen executive search firm partners, some systemizing controls over the external recruiting process, and the adoption of best practices.

Some employers have entered into preferred-supplier agreements to reduce the overall number of firms they engage and make the coordination of external search assignments more manageable and more productive. Others, including some venture capital firms, have invested in building the talent sourcing and overall executive search capabilities of their in-house recruiting or staffing teams. These teams may or may not fall within the purview of HR, which may manage external search firm engagements, and which may employ former search firm consultants.

A search consultant who specializes in conducting search assignments to fill senior HR roles says that the best leadership recruiting partnership stems from "access, communication, exchange, and trust" between the client organization's assignment stakeholders and the search consultant. "A good client values your opinion," she says, and a bad client creates a moving target, forgetting or changing entirely the initial, mutually agreed-upon job specification well into the search.

One person who appreciates both the challenge of executive recruiting and the need for better overall relations between search consultants and corporate HR officers is Janet Jones-Parker, managing director of Jones-Parker Starr, a Chapel Hill, North Carolina–based consulting firm, and former president of the Association of Executive Search Consultants.

Jones-Parker, known to those in the business as the "recruiter's recruiter" and the doyenne of finding search consultants for executive search firms and corporate staffing positions, says that forging partnerships between external search consultants and in-house management recruiting teams is a win-win for all concerned and a key lesson for executive search consultants.

"Decisions to use internal versus external resources should be part of an overall strategic plan to meet corporate hiring goals now and in the future," Jones-Parker says. "Certain assignments need to be outsourced due to confidentiality, objectivity, market access, or other special situations," she explains. "In-house recruiting teams and external search consultants need to find the path to partnership so that assignments which are conducted externally are well managed through a continuous flow of information and feedback." The key, Jones-Parker adds, is for corporations to have "a formal system for tracking internal and external recruiting activities."

That's especially relevant when one considers that HR executives sometimes find themselves stuck in the middle of organizational dysfunction and miscommunication. For example, take the case of two divisions of the same company hiring two different search firms to conduct the same search assignment. It's also true when HR executives find themselves pigeonholed or bullied by more senior management into using the same search consultant or search firm, regardless of past performance.

THE EXECUTIVE RECRUITING CYCLE

Responsibility for tracking leadership recruiting activities spans the full course of the executive recruiting cycle. That cycle extends from job specification setting and search strategy, through the selection and engagement of a search firm or the assignment of an internal recruiter to lead the search, to candidate sourcing, assessment, reference and background checking, and eventually to final negotiation, making an offer of employment, and onboarding the new executive.

And the HR executive has many roles to play, according to longtime HR executive Lucien Alziari, whose most significant HR leadership experiences were shaped during his tenure at PepsiCo and Avon Products:[4]

- Project manager
- Process owner
- Keeper of the flame (from company culture to performance standards)
- Internal influencer
- Source of insight
- Creative problem solver
- Negotiator
- Face of the company

Relations between HR departments and executive search consultants are critical, because neither can maximize their contribution to organizational performance without working effectively and collaboratively with the other. Each is to the other a powerful potential partner in shaping corporate culture, driving organizational performance, and maximizing shareholder return on investment.

"I believe that what is needed is a reevaluation of, and greater investment in, the relationship between search firm and client by both parties so that the outcome is improved performance and behavior on both sides," Peter Felix, CBE, president of the Association of Executive Search Consultants, once wrote.[5] "This is the only way to achieve truly effective management consulting."

Felix, a former executive search consultant who has also served as CEO of the British-American Chamber of Commerce, says that client relationships for a large number of executive recruiters were once rather comfortable and benign. "You had a relationship based on a partnership with your client. [It] was a bit one-sided. The client tended to accept what the search consultant said or never questioned their advice. But this was true of other consultants and professional service providers. Up through the 1980s, you never questioned your doctor, your lawyer, your accountant, your executive search consultant, but all that has changed." Over the last ten years, he adds, "the variability of the relationships have increased dramatically."

Up through the 1980s, you never questioned your doctor, your lawyer, your accountant, [or] your executive search consultant.

Felix says that executive search consultants need to reestablish the relationship with hiring organizations, a challenge he terms as "possibly one of the biggest challenges facing the executive search [profession]." The task still somewhat undone, he says, is to "make the client understand the value they're getting and we've not done a good job at that. We've got to get better at that—spelling out what you are getting. You're not just getting a placement. There's a lot more to it."

Search consultants can demonstrate real value and potential, he says, by specifically outlining, "what my expertise consists of" and sharing views with clients "on competition, compensation, and employer brand/image, trends, what we're seeing, what's happening in the market and how we perceive your attractiveness as an employer of top-grade executive talent."

Because of that market insight, Felix contends, "[Executive search consultants] are able to work with you more strategically. . . . We need a restatement of value and to get better at selling. Search consultants need to impart value, acting more as a consultant and sounding board. . . . We insist on a consultative relationship because that's the only way we'll work as a consultant. We've just forgotten how to say all that."

"Partnership with HR is crucial going forward," Felix points out, because "it's the client making the selection as well" and further because "this is a collaborative consulting process."

Ideally, the search consultant's role is to be an ally of HR and to make HR look good to the boss. And it's important for HR executives to remember that the engagement of executive search consultants—like them or not—helps legitimize and validate the promotion of internal leadership candidates.

At its core, says Leon Farley, a retired leadership recruiter who has also served as president of the Association of Executive Search Consultants and received its lifetime achievement award, the involvement of search consultants in the management succession process lends it credibility. "They're a necessary part in a process."

To win broader respect from their client partners, Farley says, executive search consultants must be highly intelligent and truly earn a hiring organization's trust by bringing to that process an ability to understand people and the context of the working environments in which they have previously operated. "Clients need a depth of analysis," he says, "and search consultants need to be experts at getting intimate with people to understand their fit for the role. They need to be compassionate and care basically about people instead of just thinking which candidate is saleable to a client. They need to be a lay psychologist, almost to the point of being offensive, like when asking a candidate, 'Tell me something about your early life.'"

Farley, who worked in a variety of management roles for ITT, Ford, and Hughes Aircraft before venturing into executive search in 1972, says he believes HR should "use the wisdom and knowledge of the HR field to choose the right search firm" and then play a very important "facilitating role" to track and communicate the progress of the search assignment and enable the kind of scheduling with senior management that it requires. "I favor a strategic HR executive being a real counsel to top management," Farley says, adding that, to produce outstanding results in an external search, "I think the fundamental relationship should be between the search consultant and the line client."

Sometimes, HR leaders bring their best executive search consultants along with them as they move from one unit of the company to another. And sometimes the search consultant recruits an HR leader who might have been a client in the past. Significant partnership between HR and the executive search consultant is not only plausible but now a true organizational mandate, given the rigorous demands of global enterprise and the intensifying competition for leadership advantage.

The late Peter Bennett, who was for many years one of the leading executive search consultants in the Asia-Pacific region, described the symbiotic relationship required for excellence in executive-level recruiting as "a two-sided arrangement," adding, "The client's approach to this association influences the speed and outcome of the search process. The single most important factor is for the client to *understand the process and their part in it.*"[6]

While one wonders how existing client partnerships (or the lack thereof) would be different if HR felt it could truly trust the executive search consultant, another forward-looking search consultant sees the fruits of collaboration in a shared mission: "I view my job as helping that hiring manager deliver on their performance objectives, and that ought to be HR's job, too."

9

EXECUTIVE SEARCH AS THE KEY TO LEADERSHIP DIVERSITY

> If more women and minorities become gatekeepers to the management succession process, other women and minorities will have more opportunities to compete for and assume positions of corporate executive leadership.
>
> CHERYL COAN, PROFESSOR OF ORGANIZATIONAL LEADERSHIP, GONZAGA UNIVERSITY AND MARQUETTE UNIVERSITY

Women and minority executives around the world are still trying to shatter the glass ceiling and improve their representation in corporate leadership positions. To help make that happen, they need to encourage more women and minorities to pursue careers as executive search consultants.

THE GATEKEEPERS

Executive recruiters sit in a remarkably powerful position to influence the gender, cultural, and overall demographic profile of C-level leaders, senior management teams, and corporate and not-for-profit boards of directors. They are the gatekeepers of executive career opportunity. And that's especially critical, given the findings of a 2007 Accenture survey that women executives say their gender is still their biggest hurdle to career advancement.[1]

The lengths to which executive recruiters will go to advocate the recruitment and eventual hiring of more highly qualified women and minorities and also to hire more diverse business professionals into their own firms will in large part set the pace for any future transfer of corporate authority to a new, more inclusive, and perhaps more globally sensitive generation of corporate leaders.

Many corporate HR leaders are waging campaigns to convince senior management of the merit of investing in leadership development and diversity recruiting programs. Few in HR, however, truly understand how executive search consultants operate as external ambassadors of corporate culture and identity. And far fewer are doing anything more than just expressing a preference that women and minority candidates be considered or included on recruiter short lists for executive appointments.

A small number of companies do offer diversity bonuses to executive search consultants whose candidate sourcing, due diligence, and effective courtship of women and minorities result in their inclusion on final candidate slates or their eventual hiring. By and large, however, corporate employers aren't paying appropriate attention to the actual makeup of executive search firms to ensure that those consultants' reach into the executive talent market is broad and truly inclusive. And this is a look that hiring corporations need to take if they are genuinely committed to increasing the diversity of their executive management team and reflecting the makeup of the markets they serve in their own workforce.

"They're saying they want diverse candidate slates but they're not yet saying the search firm has to be diverse," Barbara Provus, who retired after twenty-five years of work as an executive search consultant, says of even those corporations that have made a significant commitment to workforce and management diversity. As a result, executive search consulting firms have been lagging on the diversity front because they have faced no significant pressure from the hiring organizations that pay their fees to diversify their own staff.

Of course, increased diversity in the business world can't be measured or achieved without also considering the inclusion of a whole range of people, including those challenged by a physical handicap or infirmity, or by prejudice based on their race, religion, skin color, nationality, or sexual orientation. One of the challenges of discussing diversity in executive search consulting itself is that startlingly little information is to be found anywhere about minority representation in the profession. It simply hasn't been studied enough.

Not all companies are asleep at the switch when it comes to recognizing executive recruitment's role and potential in achieving workforce balance and inclusion. An investment bank's announcement of its appointment of an in-house executive search consultant quoted its head of investment banking as saying, "This position is critical to the development of the Corporate and Investment Bank in terms of maximizing our ability to recruit people of all backgrounds in senior roles."

Some search consultants have made the point that every search assignment is a diversity search. This is becoming a mandate, partly because some client organizations have made diversity hiring an imperative and partly because globalization is forcing a broader, more inclusive search for talent. It will eventually become the norm.

They're saying they want diverse candidate slates but they're not yet saying the search firm has to be diverse.

"MEN ARE FROM MARS . . . "

Former Harvard University president Lawrence H. Summers sparked significant controversy in January 2005, when he told an economic conference that "innate" differences between men and women may explain why more women haven't succeeded in science and math careers. Summers announced fourteen months later that he would step down, avoiding a potential faculty vote of no confidence, and Harvard immediately mobilized a search committee to find its twenty-eighth president. The exhaustive search ended in February 2007, when Drew Gilpin Faust was named president, becoming the first woman to lead the university in its 371-year history.

Some executive search consultants have accounted for their own experiences by incorporating gender-oriented practices or advancing discussion of their observations of the gender divide into their approach to the business of recruiting leadership talent. One search firm requires that all short-list executive candidates be interviewed separately by two consultants, a man and a woman. A candidate is advanced through to a client interview only if the consultants' reports of their respective interaction with that individual match up and don't raise any red flags. One explanation offered for this approach is that male search consultants tend to insert too much of their own personality, bias, comment, and judgment into the candidate interviewing process, while female search consultants tend to listen more actively and attentively, gather more information, and reserve judgment about a candidate's fit with the job opportunity.

"The difference in leadership style between men and women starts with listening," according to the findings of one joint study by Caliper, a Princeton, New Jersey–based management consulting firm, and Aurora, a London-based firm concerned with advancing women and building women's networks.[2] The same study found that women executives engender "an inclusive leadership style that starts with questions and leads to discussions."

Richard Hagberg, a psychologist and president of Hagberg Consulting Group, which conducted a study of essential manager qualities, told CareerJournal.com, "The best leaders have figured out that you get things done through other people. They see themselves as representing the interests of the people they lead. Women fit that profile perfectly."[3]

And that's especially true if working habits are any indication of women's qualifications to lead. An ExecuNet bulletin released in 2001 reported that women executives in the United States worked 57.3 hours per week, and that 26 percent of responding women executives then considered themselves workaholics, a self-identity they share with most male executives.[4]

The president of one of the oldest brand names in the executive search consulting business has said he believes executive search firms need to be more diligent in their hiring and that women may indeed be better suited to the task of leadership recruiting (or at least to the management interviewing process) than their male counterparts. He contends that women search consultants are more adept in interviews because, unlike many of their male counterparts, who tend to dominate interviews and therefore skew the takeaways, they engage in active listening during the candidate interview and thereby get a truer view of the individual.

Support for increased representation of women in top management jobs and in corporate boardrooms has grown steadily in recent years, but the realization of significant increases lags far behind. A study completed in 2006 by Catalyst, a leading research and advisory organization working with businesses and the professions to build inclusive environments and expand opportunities for women at work, found that at the current rate of change, it could take women forty-seven years to reach representation parity with men as corporate officers of Fortune 500 companies. The organization's "Census of Women in Fortune 500 Corporate Officer and Board Positions" study found that women then held just 15.6 percent of Fortune 500 corporate officer positions, down from 16.4 percent a year earlier. Further, it found that women held only 14.6 percent of all Fortune 500 board seats, compared to 14.7 percent the previous year. Catalyst also predicted that it could take women seventy-three years to reach compensation parity with men in the boardrooms of Fortune 500 companies.[5] But that assumes steady growth in women leaders' representation in those top jobs rather than the drop seen in the 2006 data.

One promising revelation from the Catalyst study was that the percentage of women who chair nominating/governance and compensation board committees had increased to about 15 percent and 10 percent, respectively, suggesting that the interaction between powerful women executives and executive search consultants would inevitably increase.

But women's access to corporate leadership positions is far more restricted in certain industries, such as the oil and gas industry, and in certain industrialized nations, such as Japan—and far more open in others, such as Norway, which, in 2003, became the first country in the world to introduce legislation stipulating balanced gender representation on company boards.[6]

CRACKING THE GLASS CEILING

The glass ceiling that continues to separate women, minorities, and other traditional outsiders from the corporate leadership structure persists in part because corporate boards and senior executives have so narrowly defined the professional experience, education, and credentials required to assume top leadership positions. Most of the largest corporations in the world are unwilling to recruit or promote someone into a very senior leadership position, such as CEO, who hasn't already held the same C-level title. As a result, many CEOs and their search consultant cronies continue to bemoan the dearth of women and minority candidates. Because so few women and minorities have been given the opportunity to lead in the C-suite, most of the apparent candidates for board and C-level posts have profiles that mirror those of the current board and CEO.

It comes as no surprise that women "occupy only a tiny fraction of the nation's very top jobs," write Irene Padavic and Barbara Reskin, because the older white male power structure continues to perpetuate long-held biases, cronyism, and homogeneity. They point out that "a large body of social psychological research indicates that people tend to prefer others from their own group."[7]

Women's leadership abilities and their growing influence in the global economy should combine to add a few more cracks in the glass ceiling. But that barrier will not be shattered until more of the older white men who control the vast majority of corporate interests around the world make more of a leadership investment in people whose backgrounds, experiences, and lives do not mirror their own. And even then the process of executive succession will remain complicated and influenced by the biases, self-interest, boardroom politics, and ever-present temptation to fall into a herd mentality of those senior executives—most often including the CEO and board members—who must ultimately pass judgment on the individuals who rank on an executive search firm's short list.

Demographic shifts alone will gradually help break the glass ceiling, as women, cultural minorities, and generally younger executives replace men from majority social and racial groups. A new generation of business executives may be more sensitive to women's issues, having built careers in a more culturally diverse workforce than their predecessors. Some have seen women begin to earn more college degrees than men (at least in the United States). And many young men have been more actively involved as nurturers and emotionally connected role models in the lives of their children than their fathers were, in part because their wives are likewise balancing the demands of work outside the home and family.

Perhaps no one understands the executive search profession's potential to accelerate senior leadership diversity better than Richard V. Clarke. A trustee emeritus with the Metropolitan Museum of Art in New York City, Clarke retired in 2005 after working nearly half a century in retained executive search consulting as president of Richard Clarke Associates, which he founded in 1957. As the dean of African American search consultants in the United States, he recruited management talent for companies such as NYNEX and Lockheed Martin. He recalls a time, especially early in his executive search career, when he saw too many other African Americans choosing careers that represented the best of only a very limited number of opportunities.

"I saw so many people taking jobs that were far less than their capabilities," Clarke says. "In the black community there's an old adage: teaching, preaching, and social work. But these were the opportunities they had because there was no interest in the corporate side in women and minorities."

Some of his most meaningful work was for corporations such as Xerox, Polaroid, and his favorite client, IBM. "These were companies that didn't have the rust-belt mentality. They were starved for new, bright talent, so they had to open the doors to people they had not recruited before."

Clarke says there is no doubt that the diversification of the executive search business would have a profound diversifying impact on senior management leadership. "We would have more women and minorities at the upper levels of corporations, the federal government, and other places because people react to examples. The more they see, the easier it becomes. . . . They'd become a valued source of people for companies who may be looking for minority candidates." After all, Clarke adds, "If you're in the market for duck, you wouldn't go to a fish store."

Executive search consultants are "the gatekeepers to opportunity for women and minorities," Clarke says, and he acknowledges that their influential roles "developed out of a desire by corporations to diversify" their increasingly global workforces. "In the final analysis, they go to the gatekeepers because they can speak frankly with the gatekeepers. Ambiguity is sometimes a shield for discrimination. Companies have to be comfortable enough to say it like it is."

The diversification of the executive search business would have a profound diversifying impact on senior management leadership.

TOWARD A MORE INCLUSIVE EXECUTIVE SEARCH PROFESSION

A friend of mine once told me about the time she was interviewed by a woman employed as a consultant with a well-known executive search firm. During their conversation, the recruiter confided how at first her male colleagues received her rather coolly, immediately assuming she was a new secretary. That treatment continued until she understood just how important her image and outward expressions of her success were to winning their respect, or at least recognition that she had earned the right to be there. "All it took was her buying a fur coat to be taken seriously by the men in the firm," this friend recalls.

That story would have come as somewhat of a surprise if executive search consultants weren't so accurately described as being overly focused on personal image or weren't engaged in a business dominated by middle-aged Caucasian men.

Women have made significant strides in executive recruiting since 1978, when inveterate executive search profession gadfly Jim Kennedy published his first list of women in the profession. Kennedy's 1982 study revealed that women's representation among the key principals in the offices of North American search firms had risen to roughly 12 percent. And by the publisher's own count, that percentage nearly doubled by 1991, rising to 22.5 percent.[8] (Kennedy's studies excluded the candidate research function, where women have been far better represented.)

The 2007–2008 edition of *The Directory of Executive Recruiters,* published by Peterborough, New Hampshire–based Kennedy Information, reveals that of the 6,630 principals identified by the North American retained executive search consulting firms profiled, 2,141—or 32 percent of the total—were women. The same Kennedy "Red Book" directory also shows that of the 2,741 principals identified as the leaders of those firms, 627, or nearly 23 percent, were women. Many of the world's best executive search consultants are women. They have demonstrated that women can succeed in executive search and they are mentoring younger women as they build their own search careers.

While women have made impressive strides in executive search (at least in North America), the same can't be said for minorities, who continue to be a very small number of the partners and consultants of most executive search consulting firms.

In the United States, "We don't have very many African Americans, Hispanics, and Asian Americans involved in the business, particularly at the partner level," observes retired search consultant William H. "Mo" Marumoto. Marumoto, president and CEO of the Asian Pacific American Institute for Congressional Studies, a nonprofit, nonpartisan educational organization, says more women have been brought into and have advanced much farther in the executive search business than have members of cultural minority groups. Marumoto agrees that a more inclusive executive search profession would have a significant diversifying effect on corporate management, "particularly at the board level."

Still, retired search consultant Richard V. Clarke says he's encouraged not only by the opportunities being presented to women and minority leadership candidates but also by the real potential for the executive search business to accelerate the diversification of corporate senior management, and for women and minorities to thrive in it. "[Executive search is] a really great business," Clarke says. "It's a relationship business first of all and if you don't establish relationships that are continuous, you can get disappointed early on," he adds. "People tend to reach out to people they know, and that socialization is part of their success. You can't just hang up a shingle. You have to develop relationships. This is a trust business."

Beyond the scope of gender and race, other groups are outsiders to the executive search career path. Executive search insiders would be hard-pressed to identify a single physically challenged executive search consultant. And there are only a few openly gay or lesbian leadership recruiters to be counted among the profession worldwide.

And what of those from underprivileged backgrounds? Just how many leadership roles in executive search consulting will open up for graduates of academic institutions outside "the Ivys" and other business schools identified by various media as elite? Given the educational backgrounds and careers of some of the most accomplished executive search consultants, no one could say that the Harvard graduate will necessarily be a better executive recruiter than someone who graduated from a lesser-known institution.

Deciding who leads is a critical task shared by executive search consultants and their client organizations, but deciding who should get a chance to contend for a top corporate job rests mostly in the hands of the searchers. That's why it's extremely important that women and minoritity search consultants urge other women and minorities to consider a career in the field, where their efforts to uncover talent and provide new opportunities to people from nontraditional leadership talent pools can go a long way. But diversification won't happen unless executive search consulting firms hire more women and minorities and corporations realize that search firms' own demographics may skew candidate slates or limit their ability to connect with top diversity candidates.

Barbara Provus, who first learned the executive search consulting business inside Booz Allen Hamilton, cautions that the women and minority search consultants of the future should be careful not to let any personal diversity agenda cloud their sourcing and engagement of management candidates. She recalls tackling a couple of executive search assignments for a particularly thrifty client who once told her, "You'll never be successful in search if you only introduce female candidates." Provus replied, "If you offer to pay more [in salary and benefits], I could attract more men."

Deciding who should get a chance to contend for a top corporate job rests mostly in the hands of the searchers.

She adds: "He perceived that my agenda was only to recruit women." But Provus estimates that no more than 20 percent of the executives she recruited during her quarter century in senior management search were women. While she advises that diversity "can't be your agenda" if you're a search consultant, many proponents of organizational diversity would undoubtedly see some benefits in further diversification of the executive search profession.

10

HOW TO ENGAGE EXECUTIVE SEARCH CONSULTANTS

An educated consumer is our best customer.

SY AND MARCY SYMS (IN COUNTLESS TELEVISION COMMERCIALS)

For more than forty years, Secaucus, New Jersey–based Syms Corp. (NYSE: SYM) has been committed to giving its customers real deals on real designer clothes. As a representative of more than two hundred authentic designer and brand names in clothing and shoes for men, women, and children, the company offers first-quality, in-season merchandise.

Syms operates a chain of close to forty stores across the United States, from New England through the Mid-Atlantic states to the Midwest, as well as in the southeast and southwest regions of the country. Many Americans shop in Syms stores each year. But many more Americans know the company for the powerful and memorable slogan that Sy and Marcy Syms have uttered in seemingly every single one of their commercials for decades: "An educated consumer is our best customer."

AN EDUCATED SEARCH FIRM CONSUMER

If being an educated consumer is important when shopping for clothes, it should be a paramount concern for an employer shopping for an executive search consulting firm. Educated consumers know full well about value and why it may require them to pay more to get more.

The selection of an executive search consultant and the commitment to be a partner in that process are just as important to the hiring organization as is the courtship of the exceptional leadership candidate; they set the stage for effective recruiting and realizing a significant return on investing in executive talent.

One common mistake that hiring companies make is basing the search firm engagement decision solely on a firm's having recently conducted almost the exact same search for another client. That qualification often guides such decisions because the search firm recently sourced candidates who may appear to the employer to embody a ready-made short list for its next management hire. But employers should think twice before hiring candidates who were recently dismissed from another employer's search.

Picking the right executive search consultant or search firm is critical to your management recruiting success, especially given the tremendous cost of a bad executive hire. But the truth is that boards and CEOs sometimes spend more time researching their choice of flat-screen, high-definition televisions than they do researching which search firms are best qualified to lead their next search assignment.

SEARCH FIRM FRIENDS AND FAMILY

Making the best choice requires some research and due diligence, because although the executive search business should be a meritocracy, it isn't.

Jim Pappas heads corporate staffing at Barnes Group (NYSE: B), a diversified international manufacturer of precision metal components and assemblies and a distributor of industrial supplies. The first thing he did when he assumed his duties as the company's relationship manager (in charge of working with executive search firms) was to, as he describes it, "eliminate the friends-and-family plan." That is, he put a stop to the practice of engaging search consultants because they were neighbors, childhood friends, relatives, old fraternity pals, or people a little too personally connected to one or more of the company's employees (perhaps having placed them in the past).

Being an educated consumer and knowing how to select, engage, and partner with an executive search consultant is crucial, in part because of the mess companies often find themselves in when a search goes wrong. You have to apply a rigorous and easily repeatable process to the task is key because you'll pay otherwise.

In the world of executive search consulting, size of firm doesn't equate with quality and consistent executive search results, which means that the big names in executive search aren't necessarily the right or most valuable choice for a given corporate consumer. But they do have a decided advantage because their brands are better known than those of smaller competitors, and their calls to prospective executive candidates may be returned first.

The world's five largest retained executive search consulting firms have held their ranking for more than twenty years—an unusually long run for the biggest companies in any business—giving them the brand advantage. The rest of the executive search consulting market is highly fragmented. HR executives—by a very wide margin—say they consistently get better service from small, often specialist "boutique" search firms, but that they are often forced to work with bigger firms whose brands are better known among the most senior corporate management.

Size of firm doesn't equate with quality and consistent executive search results.

Why does this happen? Perhaps some executive search firms are repeatedly engaged—and their performance essentially ignored—because senior corporate executives simply and rather selfishly want to stay closely connected to the best-known search consultants and the "Big 5" search firms. Might they believe those branded consultants and firms are the best positioned (as with one-stop shopping) to introduce them as individuals—fully cognizant of the decline in executive tenure—to the most compelling and largest number of executive job opportunities or board posts should they be fired or decide to leave?

It appears that this "career search" approach to executive search firm selection and engagement is alive and well. It may be at least partly responsible for the ready and repeat placement of well-known corporate executives by the same executive search consultants over time. That's an interesting form of payback for all concerned, especially since what's good for the executive-level job candidate is a matter that is and should be entirely separate from what's best for a leader's organization.

OFF-LIMITS POLICIES

Surely, there is much to be said by and heard from senior executives about how they were gracefully tended by a certain executive search consultant while a candidate for the top job they currently hold. But hiring companies will never get the chance to have many outstanding candidates tended for them and introduced to them if they let their chosen search consultants dictate the candidate sourcing strategy according to where they can search for talent and where they can't.

What really matters, especially for organizations that say they're committed to diversity and recruiting from broader pools of leadership talent, is who the executive searcher can and cannot call. And that's an important consideration, given that many search consultants have adopted a "Don't Ask, Don't Tell" policy when it comes to sidestepping the important client issue of where they can and can't go in search of executive talent.

Caveat emptor has special meaning for the hiring organization about to engage an executive search consulting firm, especially if the employer doesn't want its chosen search firm to poach its leadership talent while simultaneously searching for new executive recruits on its behalf. That's why every employer organization that engages an executive search consulting firm should know about its chosen recruiting partner's off-limits or hands-off policies, which are designed for the protection of client interests, especially given search firms' unparalleled access to privileged corporate intelligence and key personnel. It's essential that the hiring company know the protection it's getting, since search consultants can be agents of critical talent infusion and also agents of organizational blood loss. "Off limits" is, after all, the executive recruiting profession's equivalent of the Hippocratic oath taken by medical doctors, who pledge, "First, do no harm."

What really matters . . . is who the executive searcher can and cannot call.

Off-limits or hands-off safeguards are essentially promises not to recruit management talent from a client organization so long as it is a client, or, in many cases, for a period of time after a search firm's last assignment on behalf of that employer. Some of the largest search firms have in recent years turned the original intent of that search industry tenet into a source of profits by offering what amounts to "protection"—promising not to unleash recruiters on large corporations that rely on their ability to retain executive employees whose patents, profile, and raw talents contribute millions to the bottom line. Many corporations, in turn, have engaged those firms simply to be defined as clients, thereby protecting some of their best human assets. But since the search firms still need to search, off-limits agreements have recently become increasingly narrow, covering perhaps only a certain division or business unit within the corporation.

The off-limits or "client blockage" issue is an especially important consideration, as some of the largest search firms count as clients more than five thousand organizations worldwide. So the matrix of talent protection agreements they've promised (or should have promised) those client employers should pose some very valid concerns for the next potential client who seeks the widest possible access to the best senior leadership talent.

The well-known vice chairman of one global executive search firm admits, "The single biggest operational issue we have is the off-limits issue, because it prevents us from going after a lot of the best and the brightest. The more business we get, the more talent is blocked for us."[1]

Publisher Jim Kennedy would have agreed, as he once wrote: "If 'off-limits' is strictly observed, it sets a ceiling on large firm size." And, he added, "Large firms are harder to manage."[2] What's more, cautioned *Forbes* magazine, in sizing up the growth-inhibiting impact of the executive search profession's adoption of off-limits policies, "The largest recruitment firms are handicapped in doing the very job for which they are hired."[3]

But Frederick W. Wackerle, a former CEO and boardroom recruiter and author of *The Right CEO: Straight Talk About Making Tough CEO Selection Decisions,* says of off-limits policies, "It's not a big firm versus small firm issue. It's a practice issue." Wackerle worked for more than forty years as a search consultant, recruiting CEOs, directors, and senior executives. He received a lifetime achievement award for his work before he transitioned to serving as an adviser to boards and chief executives on management succession, including the role of the search consultant. He says, "The off-limits issue is something that most boards and CEOs have not even thought about. There is a considerable lack of understanding and knowledge in terms of who is doing what in the executive search community." Yet when it comes to choosing an executive search consultant, Wackerle says, "The one question that every client should ask every search consultant before every search begins is 'Who are you prevented from approaching?'"

ACCESS TO TALENT

It's imperative that hiring organizations to understand how access to talent should frame the rules of engaging executive search consulting firms. A talent acquisition leader with one large employer says understanding just how far and wide a search firm can look for a company's next leadership hire is key to a successful search: "Their ability to reach is critical to our decision about which search firm to select."

But one paradox unique to the executive search consulting business is that a firm's reach isn't the same as its access to talent. Technology has expanded the reach of most executive search consultants across the world, but given that each has a different client list, the question of which organizations they can actually recruit senior leadership candidates from must be raised before each search assignment. The vital difference between consultants' reach and their true access to executive talent is often lost on even the most experienced business executives, including a startling majority of CEOs and board directors.

The off-limits issue is something that most boards and CEOs have not even thought about.

Take the case of the corporate executive staffing leader who recommended that his client executive vice president engage one of three search firms featured on a short list of firms capable of conducting a certain search assignment. The EVP chose to engage the one global firm that was listed, because, she reasoned, "I myself would return their call first." What's entirely lost in this kind of uneducated approach to search firm selection is the fact that what moves a candidate to return a phone call to a particular name brand with significant reach is one thing, but that the same firm's access to talent is the crux of the value proposition from the corporate employer perspective. Would the search firm allow itself to make the call in the first place?

The more one knows about executive search consulting, the more one learns that maximum talent access trumps maximum talent reach. Two separate firms with equal reach may not have the same ability to recruit from the organizations in which they find target management candidates because one or more of those companies may currently be a client of one of the involved search firms.

It's important to understand how the search consultant will source talent and where the best candidates are likely to come from. But given the difficulty of recruiting senior management (even when a glut of candidates may appear to make that task easier), it's also important to not rush the search assignment. It's far better to make the right executive hiring decision and to get it right in the long run than to rush a misfit executive into a role to shave a few weeks off what is typically about a four-month process.

It's especially critical that your company truly understands how effectively your chosen search firm is serving as an ambassador of the company's brand, culture, and ethics throughout the recruitment process, from the courtship to interviewing and finally to closing the deal. Surprisingly few corporate brand managers have any idea of how their company and brand are being conveyed to the external senior management market by executive search consultants.

THE HAZARDS OF DUPLICITY

Executive search is very much an information business, and access to top management talent often hinges on a recruiter's ability to gain access to information, whether it be a corporate organization chart, the e-mail address of a senior executive, the name of an executive's personal executive assistant, or some insight into the best time to make a phone call. It is vital that your company understands how the information is being obtained and used.

Access to information was central to Hewlett-Packard's decision in recent years to engage private investigators to get to the bottom of how sensitive insider intelligence might have been leaked by a member of its board of directors. But the company apparently was unaware of the way those investigators would conduct their job and that they would resort to obtaining the personal phone records of board members under false pretenses—through a practice called *pretexting*—and filtering journalists' trash in a bid to identify the source of the leaks.

Those tactics prompted state and federal investigations, subjected top HP officials to an embarrassing public grilling by a congressional panel, and forced the resignation of several executives, including board chair Patricia Dunn, who pleaded not guilty to charges of felony fraud and identify theft brought against her in California. (The charges against her were eventually dismissed.)

The practice of *rusing* is the executive search business equivalent of pretexting. It has been around for years, and, much in the same way

HP's private investigators used pretexting to access private phone records, it is carried out by unscrupulous recruiters who glean information about a target executive under false pretenses.

One recruiter has acknowledged hiring unemployed actors to play a misleading part ever so convincingly because of the value of the information they can acquire from unsuspecting executive gatekeepers and those who may surround a sought-after leader.

Most companies—even the largest—have little understanding of the tactics their own internal executive staffing and talent sourcing teams are employing to source and later recruit talent away from direct competitors, much less their external search consultants. For a lot of reasons an organization's general counsel and chiefs of privacy, HR, and security would know well, it's vital for the company to understand how its internal and external agents are sourcing talent on its behalf. Be sure you understand and approve of the way executive recruiters—and any independent contract researchers they may use—are identifying, approaching, interviewing, and assessing potential senior management hires.

The lesson here: Make sure your organization doesn't engage in rusing, and be sure the search consultants it may retain don't either. In fact, along with a lot of other important questions I've outlined here, hiring organizations should ask how external search consultants source and approach talent.

ASK BEFORE YOU ENGAGE

It's imperative to be an educated consumer when it comes to selecting and engaging search consultants. Your organization only invites trouble if it doesn't bring some intelligence and sophistication to the process. That means researching a firm's experience, reputation, and capabilities as well as those of the individual consultant who'll actually be leading your next executive search assignment. So ask before you hire. As a guideline, here are the key questions to cover.

Consultant Qualifications

- How long have you been an executive search consultant?
- How long has your firm been in business?
- How many other searches are you currently working on?
- Do you have a local office?
- How well are you known to the most exceptional candidates for this job?
- Why would they know you, your work, and your firm?
- What might they think about your brand?
- Will your work be supported by consultants in other offices?
- What kind of work did you do before you became a search consultant?
- How well do you know our company?
- Have you recruited for us before?
- What do you know about our industry and the markets we serve?
- How do top candidates for this position feel about our company's brand?
- How would you describe our organization to potential candidates?
- What do you know about the market and strategic challenges it now faces?
- Which of the search assignments you listed as relevant to your firm's experience and qualifications to conduct the search did you personally conduct?
- Who will make the first round of candidate sourcing calls?

Consultant Process and Procedure

- Will you work with us to craft the position specification and mandate?

- How do you plan to approach this specific search assignment?
- How involved will you be in this search? Who else will be involved?
- What will you expect of me and my organization during the search?
- How and where do you expect to source candidates for this assignment?
- Will you hire a contract candidate researcher to supplement your research?
- Will you interview the internal candidates we have or will identify?
- What tools, special training, interview questions and techniques, resources, and assessment instruments do you typically employ to assess leadership candidates?
- How and how often will you report your progress on the search back to us?
- Will you verify educational credentials?
- How many references will you check on our final short-list candidates?

Other Critical Considerations

- Do you have any off-limits or client blockage issues that will restrict where you can source senior management talent for our company?
- For what other companies in our industry are you conducting searches?
- Does your firm provide coaching, outplacement, or career services to executive job seekers or any other individuals?
- What are you prepared to offer as a performance and placement guarantee?

- What percentage of the candidates you expect to introduce to our company do you already know or are already known to your firm? (In other words, will the firm conduct an original search, or will it merely be pulling names from its database?)
- What is your fee and how do you bill for expenses (both direct and indirect)?
- Do you cap your fees?
- Does your firm measure the quality of its search process? If so, how?
- How have your past successes and failures informed your approach to this search assignment?
- If we need to do a replacement search, what are your terms for doing that?
- How long do you expect the search to take?
- When will we meet the first candidates?
- How are multiple hires from the same assignment billed by your firm?
- Can you tell me how and how often you inform candidates who ultimately aren't offered a position that they were not selected?
- What kind of follow-up can we expect from you after we've extended a job offer and the candidate has accepted it?

Conducting due diligence on the selection of an executive search firm will reduce the risk of hiring the wrong firm, increase the likelihood of partnering with a firm that can offer you extensive access to the executive talent market, and otherwise pay significant dividends when the newly recruited executive starts to meet and exceed key objectives.

11

BEST PRACTICES FOR SENIOR MANAGEMENT RECRUITING

Retention shouldn't start with a counteroffer to an executive who already has one foot out the door.

DAVE OPTON, CEO, EXECUNET

Effective senior management recruiting is the lifeblood of organizational change. It is an especially powerful engine for growth, and—it's worth repeating—executive search consultants sit in a uniquely pivotal position to drive, direct, and disrupt the global search for leadership advantage. Employer organizations must discern that the payoff on executive recruiting is potentially without limit when it supports an ongoing commitment to achieve and sustain a competitive market edge by creating a clear leadership advantage. That's what makes the best practices listed here genuinely timeless.

Best Practices for Corporate Senior Management Recruiting

- Understand that culture sets the table for senior management recruiting.

- Always look for an internal successor before you search outside.
- Seek referrals to maximize succession planning and clarify the search assignment.
- Insist that your executive search consultant reinvent the candidate experience.
- Know how executives succeed in your organization and recruit for its distinct leadership requirements.
- Commit to executive onboarding.
- Measure the performance of executive search consultants.
- Understand why it takes a village to recruit a new CEO.
- Build the leadership pipeline by deploying global talent scouts.

CULTURE SETS THE TABLE

The first thing to understand is that culture sets the table for senior management recruiting. Peak organizational performance begins with peak human performance. That means creating the right environment, opportunities, and mix of challenges, incentives, and working conditions to inspire people to give everything they can for the organization and thus to get the best out of everyone. It results in a consistently high-performance organizational culture, the internal brand promise of the organization.

Organizational culture is the social fabric that defines the company from the inside and enables peak performance on the outside. It predetermines in many ways the caliber of management executive who will be attracted to the company's new leadership opportunities, and it's what motivates people to thrive and gets them to stay.

Culture comprises those mostly unwritten rules of personal interaction, employee engagement, and collective mission and desired human behavior that characterize the firm. Ideally, the result is to make people feel good about their job, make customers feel appreciated, and make investors wealthier today than they were yesterday.

Organizational culture is visible in an institution's history, its rituals, the photos of company outings that adorn the hallways or break rooms. It also lives in the stories passed down from one employee to another—savored by those who remember when the company was young, or experiencing "the best of times."

Effective senior management recruiting is the lifeblood of organizational change . . . and an especially powerful engine for growth.

Corporate culture, in the words of Douglas R. Conant, Campbell Soup Company's president and CEO, is "sacred ground." Most people spend much more time thinking about and executing their work life than with their family. So it shouldn't come as a surprise that up to 40 percent of an organization's financial performance hinges on organizational climate, culture, and employee engagement—the human ingredients of corporate performance.

More than anyone else, it is the executive management leaders of an organization who shape the tone, moral example, mission statement, strategic priorities, expectations, and working conditions that define the experiences of employees, customers, shareholders, and the legions of others touched in some way by the enterprise.

Stakeholders can begin to gauge an organization's brand, performance, and management culture simply by perusing its Web site, which must project its unique value proposition along with its employee experience to be an effective recruiting tool. Leaders usually have a lot to say about branding and how the organization's image measures up on the Web, in print, and in the media.

Those introduced to a company's chief executive officer may soon learn whether that culture wisely casts the CEO as the organization's chief recruiting officer. No one should qualify for the top job in any organization without being willing and able to play a major role in building its human capital. Michael Dell, founder, chairman, and chief executive of Dell Inc., has been known to call senior management candidates to help persuade them to join the company, and his intervention has helped Dell create a leadership advantage.

Employees are also reminded of the strength or weakness of their organization by the way senior leaders are (or aren't) held accountable for their performance. Leaders must ensure that poor performers across the organization are offered feedback as well as opportunities to improve before they begin to transform and degrade organizational culture.

All these agenda items for senior management point to this truth: You simply can't achieve peak human performance without peak organizational leadership. And no matter how hard the business might try to build its leadership team, invariably, it will have to look to the external market for senior management talent that adds to the cultural identity, whatever it may be.

That necessity will invariably lead to executive search consultants. And no matter the hard work that goes into recruiting the most qualified candidate, the exercise will fail and the organization's culture will get bruised if key internal stakeholders don't ultimately base their hiring decisions on who among the outside candidates best fits with the desired culture. Bottom line: Recruit for cultural fit and ethics match first, and leadership qualifications second.

Eventually, sometime later in the executive employment cycle, even the best-matched executive managers will be tempted by the allure of another career opportunity. Quite often, it will come in the form of an intriguing phone call from an executive search consultant, a referral, or perhaps a posting on an executive networking Web site.

Consider this headline: "Nearly Half of U.S. Workers Are Expected to Search for a New Job in 2007."[1] That's according to an online survey of 5,331 employed individuals, which also revealed that two-thirds of the respondents who wouldn't actively look for new employment would nonetheless be open to considering a job change if the right opportunity knocked.

Recruit for cultural fit and ethics match first, and leadership qualifications second.

That reality underscores the importance of employee retention—and, most critically, senior management retention—as part of the organization's cultural commitment to hiring, developing, recruiting, and providing fulfillment for top performers. But much as individuals often fail to take saving for their retirement seriously, so too do many organizations overlook the importance of sound retention policies and how the lack of them increases employee turnover and inflates recruitment costs. Periodically "re-recruiting" the company's best performers is clearly an organizational best practice.

Retention shouldn't start with a counteroffer to an executive who already has one foot out the door.

These days and increasingly in the future, in an environment fraught with headlines such as "Pay Packages Now Allow Executives to Change Jobs with Less Risk,"[2] an organization simply can't win the global war for executive talent without also winning the battle to retain top management talent. As Dave Opton, founder and CEO of senior management networking community ExecuNet, has tirelessly advised corporate leaders, "Retention shouldn't start with a counteroffer to an executive who already has one foot out the door." And he adds, "Counteroffers simply don't retain people much longer."

So how can you build effective retention policies into the working environs and social fabric of the organization? A study by Ernst & Young, ExecuNet, and the Human Capital Institute found these elements among the most effective:[3]

- Flexible work schedules and flexible or special benefits
- Retention bonuses
- Phased retirement
- Mentoring

"If you're going to have a successful company, value those people who go home at night because they are the company," says Gregory Smith, an Atlanta-based author and consultant on employee retention strategies who is also president of Chart Your Course International. "A lot of executives aren't focused on the fact that the business is those human assets . . . the senior people have got to be involved in retention."[4] Smith adds: "If you have a high employee turnover rate, you're spending a lot of money unnecessarily. If you don't have your finger on the pulse of retention, your people and your profits are going out the door."

The best organizational culture sets the stage for financial performance and employee satisfaction in many ways. If you build it, talented workers, managers, and executive leaders will come. If you foster learning, teamwork, fair play, and accountability, they will thrive and bring others to the dance. And especially if you re-recruit the best of them through word and deed, they will stay—even when the going gets tough, as it sometimes does.

LOOK INSIDE FIRST

Always look for an internal successor before you search outside. When evaluating where to find the right individual to fill an executive-level job vacancy or a newly created management position, consider whether promoting a current employee is a viable option, and remember that other employees may be sitting on considerable institutional intelligence about how that person fits into the organization's culture and its business agenda.

Something else worth considering is whether the job specification for the senior management post requires someone who is a turnaround or change specialist, or someone who will simply be expected to grow the existing business, most often with preordained human assets and linear budget expectations.

Yet another issue is whether the organization can afford to engage an executive search consultant and whether it's prepared to pay the new hire what typically amounts to a 20 percent to 40 percent premium in executive compensation. That's roughly the kind of compensation increase it will take to entice a proven executive leader from outside the company to leave a current employer and join your organization. "Going outside" or "going to search" will cost you. The potential payoffs are enormous, it's true, but before your company looks outside its walls for executive talent, ask these questions:

- Should someone be promoted into the position?
- Does it make sense to offer someone a lateral move to meet the leadership need?
- Can the organization's succession plan, HR department, or any line managers provide any insight about the skills, education, and experience needed to succeed in the role?
- Have we considered potential candidates from outside the headquarters office, perhaps in a business unit based in some other country?

Assume that searching outside the organization for management-level talent should be the second option, to be pursued after an exhaustive assessment of existing leadership assets and the true challenge at hand. However, bear in mind that certain variables, such as a need for strict confidentiality, the perceived difficulty of finding an executive capable of handling the job, or the need for a strategic course correction, may prompt an external search right from the start.

SOLICIT REFERRALS

Seek referrals to maximize succession planning and clarify the search assignment. You've surely heard it before: "It's who you know." Increasingly in this technologically wired and professionally and socially networked world, it's now also "who knows you." And—given that word of mouth is probably the single most effective form of advertising—"and who's willing to tell others that they think highly of you."

Once a decision has been made to look outside the organization for a key executive recruit, the board of directors, C-suite leaders, and ultra-networked "friends of the firm"—including well-connected corporate alumni—should be approached and solicited to turn up leads on promising candidates for the job.

Smart companies, and many of those that populate the Fortune 500 and various lists identifying the best employers to work for, long ago realized the benefit of harnessing employee and alumni network referrals to satisfy their talent needs and evangelize the very best of their culture, mission statement, and employment experience. These channels can be some of a hiring organization's best avenues to new and diverse pools of talent.

Several organizations have created their own alumni clubs as a way of staying in touch and optimizing their ongoing communication with former employees. Occasionally, that leads to the hiring of a boomerang employee—one returning for a second stint with a company. Most often, it provides a way for alumni who respect and communicate with their former employer to refer talented individuals, thereby significantly increasing the corporation's network.

Smart companies . . . long ago realized the benefit of harnessing employee and alumni network referrals to satisfy their talent needs.

Employee referrals have accounted for between 35 percent and 40 percent of all "experienced" hires at Deloitte Touche Tohmatsu, the global management consultancy, according to Frank Wittenauer, Deloitte's global e-recruitment leader. He says the company wants to increase employee referrals as a percentage of new hires from about 15 percent to at least 30 percent in the United Kingdom, for example, and to as much as 50 percent of new experienced professional and management hires in places like Australia. "We have no doubt that employee referral is where the quality is," Wittenauer says.[5]

Corporate HR leaders report mostly resounding success with employee referral programs intended to identify entry-level and junior management recruits. And a study by the American Management Association found that referrals to identify prospective senior management hires are just as effective and valuable as those targeted much farther down the organizational chart.[6]

For starters, referrals by the board of directors regularly lubricate the CEO search process (which I'll discuss here shortly), aided by the social proximity of most board members to experienced corporate leaders and the ease with which someone at that level can simply introduce a potential candidate into the process.

Referrals generated by senior leaders' access to meaningful business interactions at chambers of commerce, trade associations, Rotary Club International meetings, and gatherings of other civic, business, and fraternal organizations have long primed the pump for management recruiting. Today, technology has made employment-related referrals easier and more efficient than ever. But with workforce diversity a clear priority for many organizations, it's important to broaden the scope of referral gathering so that the good word about your organization spreads on the lips of all employees and generates leads to more than just the most networked senior executive friends of the board.

The growing popularity of business and career networking sites such as LinkedIn, ExecuNet, and those hosted by the multitudes of trade associations, together with the explosive growth of so-called social networking sites like MySpace.com, facilitates such referrals at a time when most at the executive level may sense a loss of personal connectivity with friends, business associates, and others in their individual networks.

In this effort, boards can take a tip from executive recruiters, who work hard to maintain their "face time" with the key members of their networks. Executive search consultants, perhaps more than any other business professionals in the modern world, pride themselves on being in the know. They are extremely well-connected people. They are consummate social butterflies and ubernetworkers. They themselves are also especially reliant on referrals—referrals that lead them to the people their clients most want to recruit.

Those referrals lead to introductions, and those introductions lead to conversations that help executive recruiters stay acutely aware of key business leaders' willingness to consider new opportunities—often before a prospect's family and friends have any idea a change may be in the wind. Long before a high-profile executive resigns in a public statement to the board, shareholders, or the business media, chances are an executive recruiter is in the know and perhaps even directly involved in the career transition.

Leadership recruiters count on referrals to keep track of executive job movements from one company to the next, and they're also not shy about flaunting knowledge gained from a referral source, a newspaper, or a corporate filing when they happen upon someone who is in their database, but unaware of the attention. As one recruiter is fond of saying to executive management targets he meets in the course of his business, "Sure, I know who you are . . . we've been tracking you for some time."

REQUIRE PROPER CARE AND FOLLOW-UP

Insist that your executive search consultant reinvent the candidate experience. At present, search consultants' collective treatment of candidates, most notably their widespread lack of follow-up with candidates who weren't offered the job for which they interviewed, remains an Achilles' heel of the profession. It is a failing that only feeds negative corporate perceptions about "headhunters."

The seriousness of the field's everyday affairs once prompted a talented American boardroom search consultant to hand me a copy of "The Search Consultant's Prayer," a personal and professional entreaty meant to seek spiritual guidance, admit wrongdoing, and ask for the wisdom of sound judgment about executive job candidates. What resonated about that prayer were the words it used to describe the gauntlet that some senior management job candidates experience as they are engaged by the search consultant and courted toward a potential marriage with a new employer. It acknowledged that even some of the most talented candidates for corporate leadership positions are occasionally—and not exactly in this order—misled, oversold, abused, ignored, inconvenienced, and otherwise sacrificed on the altar of the executive selection process, in part because of the search consultant's indifference to what job candidates actually experience.

"We must at all times be aware of the power we have either to enhance or destroy not only an individual's career but also the lives of his family," search consultant Allan D. R. Stern once said in his opening remarks to a conference of corporate and professional recruiters.[7]

Sometimes search consultants underestimate the influence of the candidate's life partner. That lapse occasionally disrupts an otherwise masterfully executed courtship process, as when a spouse decides it's a bad idea to move, convinces the candidate that the pay or opportunity isn't worth it, or otherwise balks at a significant lifestyle change. An Accountemps survey that addressed 150 executives employed among the thousand top U.S. companies once found that 42 percent of them responded "spouse/significant other" when asked who they were most likely to approach first for the purpose of evaluating a potential job change. "Mentor" followed at 28 percent, and then "coworker" at 13 percent, "friend" at 11 percent, "other family member" at 5 percent, and "someone else" at 1 percent.[8]

Ask any executive search consultant about the treatment of executive-level job candidates and most will admit at least some level of guilt about their occasional mishandling of or failure to follow up with the also-rans in the horserace for a particular leadership opportunity. A distinguished British executive search consultant turns somewhat red-faced when, in urging his colleagues to do better, he acknowledges the "seemingly cavalier treatment of candidates."

Improving the treatment of job candidates is one challenge the global executive search profession can and should immediately tackle. There are few barriers to doing that. After all, although search consultants represent the hiring company, candidates are the essence of the search firm's business. People are the product, executive search is the process—and well served is the hiring organization whose brand and identity are fully preserved by search ambassadors who treat candidates with the utmost decorum.

Simply put, executive search consultants need to revisit the Golden Rule. Prescribing a new course of interaction with people who are still today left in the cold by the quest for world-class leadership talent, one Canadian search consultant forcefully exhorts his colleagues to "treat them the way we would want to be treated." Treating executive-level job candidates with candor, respect, dignity, and honesty (from acknowledging the unsolicited résumé from a candidate wannabe to closing the loop with a short-list finalist who didn't get the job) is perhaps the best way to leave a lasting impression with the many individuals who are in some way touched by the executive search process.

"Treating candidates with respect at all levels is important, but even more so when it comes to those who circulate at the senior end of the leadership food chain in business," says former executive search consultant Rick Helliwell, vice president of recruitment in the HR unit of Dubai-based Emirates Group. Raising the bar on how senior-management candidates are treated during the recruitment courtship process would improve outcomes, he adds, because "candidates get a refined process and a consistent high standard of handling, and they are better informed and better aligned to the business's culture before any interview time (for either party) is wasted."

Much as corporate hiring managers and search consultants are said to judge a candidate's qualifications with only a brief glance at a résumé, so too do executive job candidates judge a potential employer by the humanity that is extended (or most often not extended) by people they believe—rightly or wrongly—should give them some consideration. Going the extra mile to prove that theirs is indeed, in the words of one of the profession's founders, "the highest form of management consulting" is in search consultants' own best interests. After all, the sharpest among them already know that today's candidate is tomorrow's client, and so they acknowledge (even if only to dismiss) unsolicited résumés; they build referral networks for candidates, and they otherwise treat them with the dignity deserving of any human petitioner, let alone the most accomplished in business.

LOOK FOR PEOPLE WHO CAN SUCCEED

Know how executives succeed in your organization and recruit for its distinct leadership requirements. Ask yourself, Who are some of the best leaders in this organization? What is it that makes them so successful? Simple questions. Important answers. Answers that can go a long way toward determining just how your organization should interview and assess executive leadership candidates.

Much as the Boy Scouts and Girl Scouts have built their expected leadership dynamics into their respective oaths and ceremonies, so too should your organization establish the character and ethical dynamics against which all senior management recruits should be measured and, after they've joined your business, held accountable.

The process of organizational change often forces corporate history, ceremony, and ritual to be undone, and that requires new leadership that can push the change agenda and enlist the support of employees, who will, over time, embrace a new culture as if it has always existed. But organizational culture, whether it is reinforced or redefined under the stewardship of new executive management, should inform decisions about the kinds of leadership traits that are most desired in external management candidates. The truth is that what flies in one organization may not fly in another. If the enterprise has any recollection of past executive hiring mistakes and any sense of what it is that makes its top performers excel, it will be well served in recruiting against both the drivers and the inhibitors of success in the organization.

The new leadership mandate presented in Chapter 5 can serve as a guide, but its principles should only add to the institution's sense of which behaviors are worth rewarding and which may run counter to its best practices. At its core, leadership is about service, not entitlement. And success in top corporate management hinges on emotional intelligence, a sense of personal responsibility, and stewardship that aims at preserving the interests of shareholders, customers, and employees.

DON'T LET NEWCOMERS GO IT ALONE

Commit to executive onboarding. The process of successfully bringing in a newly recruited business executive by providing timely performance feedback is the best protection for any executive search. An organization needs a system of ropes and ladders that backs up the guidance and choice of even the best Sherpa consultant to prevent a potentially fatal high-altitude fall.

The truth is that the sink-or-swim approach to executive management integration is old school. Executive onboarding, whether perceptions about a leader's early impact are measured 60, 90, 100, or 120 days after entry into a new post, should follow every external search. As noted, smart executives are learning to demand this kind of organizational feedback as part of their employment agreements. After all, the more softly they land, the more quickly they develop momentum, build rapport, and gain confidence. Those elements move them closer to achieving objectives and finding their place in the organizational fabric.

TRACK RESULTS

Measure the performance of executive search consultants. One of the troubles with corporate executive staffing is that most employer organizations fail to learn from their mistakes. And few have demonstrated the effectiveness and long-term financial impact of their senior management recruiting.

Another common problem is approaching (and measuring) the external search for senior executive talent with the same cost-per-hire metrics that apply farther down the organizational pyramid. These metrics shouldn't guide recruitment at the executive level in the ways they do lower in the organizational talent mix because, despite the magnitude of executive search costs, the pursuit of six- or seven- or even eight-figure leadership talent needs to be approached with an eye toward the creation of shareholder value rather than the containment of costs. But that's not to say that an employer shouldn't keep tabs on the investment it is making in recruiting external management talent, or that the critical pursuit of effective leadership recruitment and succession is a domain that should be afforded an open checkbook.

Most employer organizations fail to learn from their mistakes.

Because the external search for senior management talent is about making the right investment for the future, the performance of executive search consulting firms should be measured through the long-term performance of the individuals they help place. The individual performance of externally recruited executives, overlaid against group and organizational performance, is a good indicator of search firm effectiveness.

Hiring organizations should develop the following metrics to track their executive leadership strength and the performance of their executive search partners:

- Standards and ratings to measure the caliber of the incumbent leadership team (how top leaders measure up against their own individual performance objectives)
- Number of promotions into executive-level positions versus number of external recruits into executive posts in a given year
- Tenure and performance ratings of internal executive promotions versus tenure and performance ratings of external executive hires over a three-year period
- Assessment of externally recruited executives' tenure and performance, broken out by search firm that sourced and recruited them
- Analysis of externally recruited executives' tenure and performance, broken out by source of hire (search firm placement, employee or board referral, other)
- Number of women and minority executives promoted internally versus those sourced and recruited through executive search firms

- Percentage of senior leadership positions identified in management succession plan that can be filled through internal promotion versus percentage that must be filled with external talent
- Relative bench strength and number of credible management successors developed by internally promoted executives versus those developed by externally promoted executives
- Percentage of high-performing executives and succession plan candidates recruited externally versus internally

For each executive the company hires—whether through internal promotion or external recruitment—the performance, tenure, and growth of the individual should be measured against the growth of his or her operating unit and of the organization as a whole. That essentially creates a three-dimensional snapshot from which to gauge the performance of the individual in the context of group and organizational performance and goal attainment. From that, one can begin to measure the performance of executive search firms.

Individuals' performance should be tracked by their annual performance review and any promotions, while the organization's measurements should be tracked consistently by revenue growth, earnings-per-share growth, and total return to shareholders, as Figure 2, on page 188, illustrates.

What emerges from this assessment is some perspective on how someone's performance shaped or was shaped by his or her business environment, measured at the closest unit operating level and more broadly in the context of organizational issues often outside his or her control or sphere of influence.

It's important not to measure executive performance (through performance assessment scores, promotions, and other changes in responsibility and tenure) in a vacuum, because individual motivations and goal achievement are influenced by operating group dynamics as well as overall organizational culture and performance. These variables should be taken into consideration as a hiring organization begins to assess search firm selection and engagement options. They are also important as the organization tries to measure the past performance of any search consultant or search firm. At the same time, the employer needs to look at its onboarding of an external executive hire, to see how that may have affected results.

One important external recruitment metric that shouldn't be reinvented is the time it takes to complete an executive search assignment. The average has for many years stood at about four months, perhaps a bit longer. Some corporate leaders complain that their business units aren't recruiting quality management talent fast enough, and some search firms award bonuses to their staff if a search assignment is completed in less than a hundred days, but it pays not to rush the process. The pace of global business is accelerating and the pressure to recruit a new executive is usually intense. Nonetheless, it's still far better to take a little more time to make sure you're selecting the right executive than to push ahead and hire someone despite concerns about his or her fit with the organization.

GET WHY IT TAKES MANY HANDS

You also need to understand why it takes a village to recruit a new CEO. An organization's search for a new chief executive officer is for many reasons unlike the search for any other senior management leadership post. The visibility of the CEO role, the pressures facing it, and the authority, pay, and expectations that come along with it make the job of choreographing the CEO search process extremely delicate, super discreet, and always very consequential to the future of the hiring organization and its shareholders and employees.

Screw up the search for a division director or vice president and few people outside the employer organization will notice. But if an ongoing CEO search leaks to outsiders, drags on for several months, or gets manipulated by the outgoing CEO, it could land the organization in hot water with shareholders. It might even lead to an embarrassing story in the major business media and the revelation that other compa-

FIGURE 2 **Tracking Executive Job Performance and Tenure Against Organizational Performance**

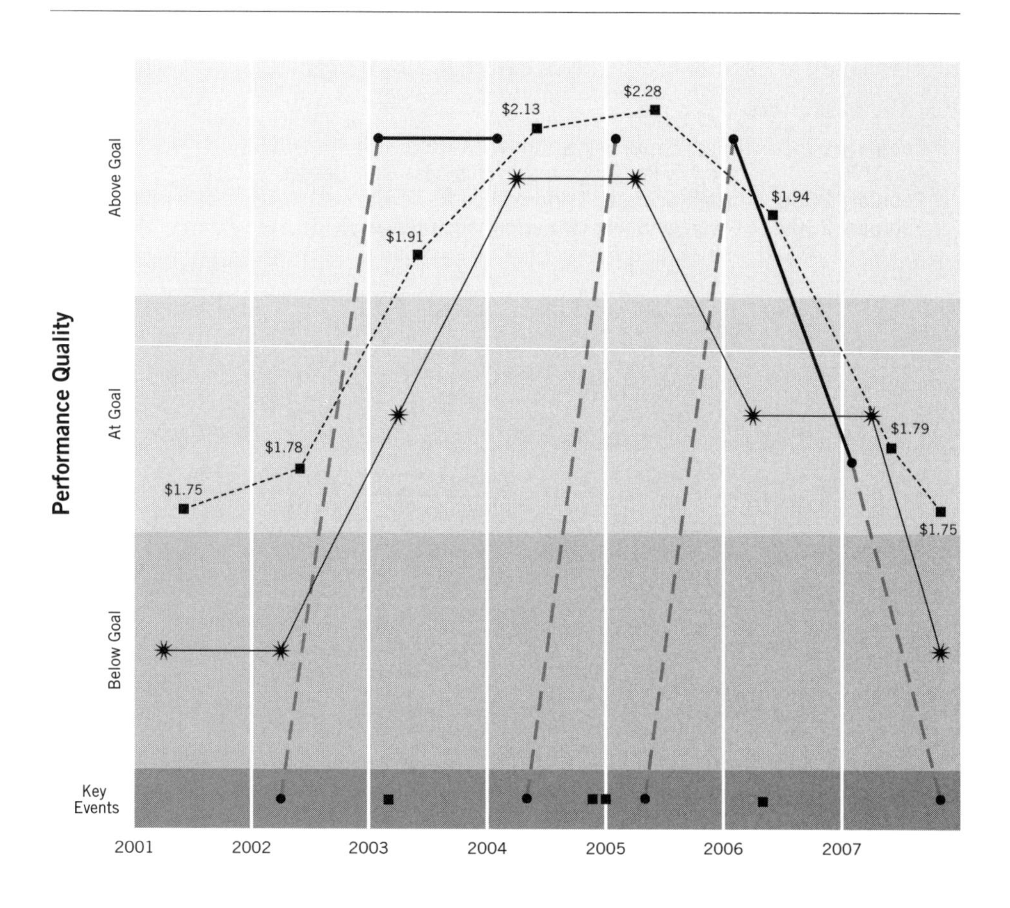

FIGURE 2 CONT'D

● **Individual Performance Points**

April 2002	Key Event: Point of Hire (External, Director of Sales, United Kingdom)
February 2003	High Score on Performance Review
February 2004	High Score on Performance Review
May 2004	Key Event: Promoted to VP of Sales, United Kingdom
February 2005	High Score on Performance Review
May 2005	Key Event: Promoted to Business Unit Leader, Europe
February 2006	High Score on Performance Review
February 2007	Average Score on Performance Review
November 2007	Key Event: Point of Exit (Resignation)

✷ **Group Performance Points**

(Note: Starts one year before exec joined; snapshot taken at executive's exit point)

April 2001	U.K Sales (Below Goal)
April 2002	U.K. Sales (Below Goal)
April 2003	U.K. Sales (At Goal)
April 2004	U.K. Sales (Above Goal)
April 2005	U.K. Sales (Above Goal)
	Europe Sales (Above Goal)
April 2006	Europe Sales (At Goal)
April 2007	Europe Sales (At Goal)
November 2007	Europe Sales (Below Goal)

■ **Organizational Performance Points**

(Note: Starts one year before exec joined; snapshot taken at executive's exit point)

June 2001	Earnings per share (EPS) of $1.75
June 2002	EPS of $1.78
March 2003	Key Event: Company marks 50 years in business
June 2003	EPS of $1.91
June 2004	EPS of $2.13
December 2004	Key Event: Company is acquired
January 2005	Key Event: Longtime CEO retires
June 2005	EPS of $2.28
May 2006	Key Event: New CEO appointed
June 2006	EPS of $1.94
June 2007	EPS of $1.79
August 2007	Key Event: New Global Sales Leader appointed
November 2007	Projected EPS of $1.75

nies' CEOs had interviewed for the position, something that might spook investors in those other companies and possibly ruin those CEOs' careers.

That particular threat exists because, unlike most of the executive searches conducted around the world each year, the search for a new CEO is a process usually controlled by powerful members of board nominating committees, who may themselves be the CEOs of other companies and who almost universally believe they may already know just the right person for the job. Increasingly, however, CEO searches will ring hollow if the slate of candidates isn't global in scope, recognizing that some of the most influential business is happening outside the traditional centers of North America and Europe.

Today, it's not uncommon to hear board members, outgoing CEOs, and search consultants lament the dearth of candidates for a CEO search. That's because boards—especially those charged with governing the affairs of the world's largest publicly traded companies—have settled into the bad habit of considering only those individuals who are or have been CEO of a similar company. That has the effect of disqualifying every living soul on the planet, save for a small and select handful whose reputations, social credentials, and backgrounds match up to those of the hiring company's board members.

And because the vast majority of big company boards are populated by older white men, the leading CEO candidates are most often other older white men. It's no wonder that so many women and minority executives have been left out of the CEO search. But that should change—in part because of studies like one conducted by Booz Allen Hamilton, the global management consulting firm, which shows "repeat CEOs" perform no better than new CEOs who have never held that title before.[9]

The role and makeup of the board of directors brings unusual potential to the artful conduct of a CEO search assignment because CEO search is one area in which board members can demonstrate the combined influence of their professional networks (if they're not too insular) and their individual contribution to the success of the company.

But for that to happen, boards have to break up the status quo when it comes to the typical CEO search process.

It's no wonder that so many women and minority executives have been left out of the CEO search.

Far too many multinational organizations leave the recruitment of a new CEO—and, for that matter, most key executive hires—*solely* in the hands of an executive search consultant. That's a recipe for disaster if the organization doesn't really get to know the person it's recruiting, or if the individual being recruited doesn't reveal true motivations during the interview process. And it's not just a remote possibility. It's been an unfortunate lesson to many organizations only after the fact, often when the fraudulent dealings of criminals in suits are revealed. Employers must consider a broader pool of potential candidates, inject more assessment into the selection of consultants, and make their work—or at least the objectivity of their work—more visible to shareholders.

"Boards are doing a terrible job and they admit it . . . in terms of management succession and finding the next CEO," says T. K. Kerstetter, president and CEO of Board Member Inc., a privately held publishing, database, research, and conference company focused on corporate board issues and governance trends.[10] Finding a solution to that mess brings a new set of challenges to the task of recruiting board members. At the end of the day, organizations must build boards that truly understand how internal climate and leadership influence performance and acknowledge that talent acquisition is perhaps a board's biggest responsibility.

It is the search consultant's interviews with board members that usually yield the highest-value targets—as many of the board members are themselves CEOs and especially well-networked individuals, both professionally and socially. If those networks are inclusive from a workforce diversity perspective, and if board members acquire the courage to consider those not already experienced in the CEO role for the top job, the board can be a compelling partner in the successful completion of a CEO search.

Nonetheless, the selection and engagement of an executive search consultant is also critical to the CEO search process. That's because if the search firm isn't similarly well-networked and willing to introduce a nontraditional candidate slate that includes women, minorities, and other dark horses whose leadership also merits serious consideration, the candidate short list might reflect only the traditional prospect profile.

So, as with the board's profile, the search consultant's profile is also usually a key determinant of what the roster of CEO candidates will look like. That's why injecting serious due diligence into the process is so important and vital to the protection of shareholder interests. That kind of due diligence—given the realities of what it costs to hire and fire a CEO—should force hiring organizations to consider why it takes a team of specialist outside consultants to "Find Jack," as the search for a new CEO was often labeled during the glory days of Jack Welch at the helm of General Electric.

The business of recruiting a new CEO is especially serious considering the authority and awesome responsibility that comes with it. Getting an organization's CEO selection decision right costs far less than fixing it after getting it wrong, and that, in part, is why the process requires the involvement of a variety of outside partners in addition to the executive search consultant:

- Executive compensation consultant
- Background-screening consultant
- Reference-checking consultant (for added due diligence)
- Specialist lawyer (who brings employment terms and contract expertise)
- Medical doctor
- Executive onboarding consultant

These additional external advisers help the organization go beyond cultural fit for the job and judge the candidate's actual fitness for it. The following sections discuss each of these roles.

Executive Compensation Consultant

An executive compensation consultant should be involved in view of the potential danger of overpaying the new hire. This specialist can also help the hiring organization create an attractive pay and benefits package and calibrate the market compensation intelligence provided by the executive recruiter. Well-planned enticement packages are what help talented CEO candidates overcome the anxiety they—and possibly their partner and children—may be feeling about leaving the comfort of their current high-paying job and social environs.

Background-Screening Consultant

However well qualified they are to conduct the search assignment, executive search specialists should not be paid or relied on to conduct background checks. The organization needs an independent and detailed report on a candidate's credit history, educational credentials, employment history, and criminal record, if there is one. The failure to thoroughly screen and otherwise substantiate a candidate's claims or the truthfulness of stories that have contributed to the candidate's reputation has led to embarrassment and ruin for many companies and CEOs around the world.

Background screening is an indispensable facet of leadership recruiting due diligence, and it is unquestionably the hiring organization's responsibility. If you'd rather not find out that a newly hired key executive has invented advanced degrees from an elite business school or failed to pay child support or filed for personal bankruptcy on several occasions or been convicted of a crime, consult with an expert in employment background screening. Many of the people working in this field have a background in law enforcement.

Reference-Checking Consultant

Reference checks also play an important role in getting to know potential CEO candidates, and it's increasingly important for everyone involved in the recruiting process to understand the importance of exploring gaps in candidate résumés. Whether conducted by the search consultant or an independent reference-checking consultant, reference checks must be built into the CEO selection process as a safeguard for the hiring organization.

Specialist Lawyer

It is very important to get an informed legal perspective on the new CEO's employment contract. That's why the hiring organization needs to hire a specialist lawyer or barrister with expertise in employment law, terms, and contracts who can advise it, or, as is sometimes the case, the CEO candidate it is courting. That's an important consideration; the hiring organization may want to assess the disengagement of its chosen CEO successor from any noncompete agreement, nonsolicitation agreement, or other restrictive employment contract.

The candidate may also need to be coached about the best wording of a resignation letter, the files that can and cannot legally be brought to the new employer's premises, and the legal obligations of all parties once the resignation letter is submitted.

Medical Doctor

An often-overlooked perspective that may be equally critical in the external recruitment of a new CEO is that of a medical doctor. The value of a complete physical exam and medical report on an executive job candidate's physical fitness, especially given the rigors of life for a twenty-first-century CEO, should not be overlooked. Peter M. Felix, CBE, president of the Association of Executive Search Consultants and a former executive recruiter, acknowledges that a medical screening is "very common" in these circumstances to assess "the health and energy of the senior executive."

An externally recruited CEO's health is, in part, an important factor because of the failure of many employer organizations to develop a coherent leadership succession plan. In this regard, multinational corporations around the world share a common problem, and one that could be remedied if only more boards of directors and sitting CEOs devoted the resources to developing such a plan. It's far better to have a contingency plan in place than to be unprepared when suddenly and unexpectedly confronted with the shocking news that the CEO has collapsed and died.

Executive Onboarding Consultant

Last but certainly not the least of these valuable outside advisers is the executive onboarding consultant. Typically experienced in the fields of psychological assessment, market research, executive recruitment, executive coaching, and organizational development, these consultants also bring a valuable outside perspective to the external recruitment of a new CEO.

The support and feedback that comes from executive onboarding is an outstanding protection for the investment represented by an external search for a world-class CEO. Every new CEO can benefit greatly from feedback—especially from the boardroom—soon after joining a new organization, and may just perform better and stay longer as a result.

To this list of external parties to the CEO selection process one can envision the eventual addition, especially in the case of publicly traded companies, of a shareholder advocacy liaison. That person might serve as an independent link between the organization's owners and all the official parties to the CEO recruitment and selection process. But it's important to note that such a role would require—as with all others involved—the utmost discretion and an ability to report on the progress or outcome of the search without giving away information that could expose the identity of candidates or otherwise impede the momentum of the search or disrupt its closure.

Mainly, it's essential to realize that, even under the best of circumstances, the best strategy for hiring the right CEO at the right time requires a team of specialist consultants, each of whom adds a valuable independent and objective perspective to the process. That's why, when it comes to making critical decisions about searching for a new CEO, it really does take a village.

BUILD A WORLD-SPANNING PIPELINE

Build the leadership pipeline by deploying global talent scouts. Much in the same way that companies should seek to tap into their employees' and alumni's networks as sources of employment referrals, so too should they tap into executive search consultants' considerable local, national, and global networks to recruit senior management talent to achieve growth objectives, build their leadership bench, or counter employee attrition. After all, the global sourcing of leadership talent remains one of the greatest human capital challenges facing many organizations, and executive search consultants are paid to know where to fish for the best leadership talent and to point their clients in the direction of the most promising talent pools.

Now and in the future, leading companies will identify, target, and connect with the most promising senior management candidates months and years before they may have a need to more formally court them, either directly or with the help and guidance of executive search consultants. Businesses need "a continuous talent drive," as one search consultant describes it. Ideally, institutions will have reached out long before their need for top leadership talent becomes urgent.

Part of what plagues corporate management succession today is the fact that many companies don't turn to the executive search consultants until they've failed on their own or otherwise feel some sense of institutional panic. Executive search consultants can serve as ambassadors of a client organization before they are actually charged with filling an immediate or pending senior management vacancy. But that requires a close, ongoing relationship between the hiring organization and the search consultant, who becomes the eyes and ears of the company and a true talent scout in the external leadership market.

Because of their 24/7 focus on the executive talent market and what moves it as well as their capacity to source talent globally, these management staffing Sherpas can lend unparalleled perspective and reach to the challenge of building an organization's leadership pipeline for the future. It's critical to "keep your pipeline full," says one top boss, because "without [talented] people, nothing else matters."

E. Neville Isdell, chairman and CEO of the Coca-Cola Company, spoke of the need for both internal and external pipeline development when he told the *Wall Street Journal:* "I have to be developing people inside the company who are capable of succeeding me, and equally I have to have a list of people from outside who I believe could come in in an emergency or somewhere down the road if they continue to be successful. We are looking at all of those options."[11]

More and more, executive search consultants and corporate talent management and talent acquisition leaders believe that success in corporate management succession is all about finding tomorrow's leaders today and engaging them well ahead of any formal recruitment approach. Ice hockey legend Wayne Gretzky once said, "I skate to where the puck is going to be, not to where it has been." That is very much the same order for business leaders connected in some way to or directly responsible for managing the search for game-changing executive talent. The search for a new CEO should be global in scope, especially for any enterprise that does business internationally, and hiring organizations should be prepared to skate wherever they need to—anywhere in the world—to connect with potential future leaders.

As companies compete in a global race for innovation, they are also increasingly engaged in a global race to be the first to connect with the great minds, master tacticians, and other exceptional leaders who will eventually be the most sought-after external management candidates.

The pressure to exploit new and emerging markets and establish stronger footholds in key locations is already driving some corporate employers to accelerate their business development and management staffing capabilities by recruiting teams of talented individuals. John Sculley, the former Apple Computer CEO, once told me: "I spend more of my time recruiting the best teams, because the companies with the best teams win. In a world where everything is commoditized, the difference is the quality of your team and ability to differentiate."

But the increasing frequency of such group recruiting initiatives—a practice executive search consultants have dubbed "liftouts"—also presents the very real threat of companies' having to replace an entire team of talented sales executives, designers, intellectual property experts, or others whose departure will invariably diminish a product or knowledge advantage over the competition.

Steven L. Manchel, an attorney with Manchel & Brennan in Newton, Massachusetts, represents companies intent on hiring high-performance teams and also those seeking a legal remedy to the hurt they've felt from the liftout of groups of key employees. "Five years ago, it was called a raid," he says. "With 'liftouts,' the recruiters have come up with a tagline that sanitizes what's going on. But these liftouts will unquestionably increase in frequency and use because of the industry consolidation taking place and the way companies are structuring themselves internally."

In a world where everything is commoditized, the difference is the quality of your team and ability to differentiate.

Manchel says that consolidation in a number of industries is creating larger, more focused work groups (whose members may or may not be bound by non-compete agreements), and that these teams are more portable than they've ever been before and "easier to identify and remove as a unit." Liftouts have already become more prevalent because of "the continued collapsing of competition and the increased use of group or unit approach to the task," Manchel says, and "companies need to be prepared to hire groups and lose groups, because that's where recruiting is going."

Of course, to understand the enterprise's long-term external management talent needs, one must also appreciate how its current high-potential employees, its top-performing employees, and its ready-now leadership successors already fit into its talent-mapping plans. Baseball great Branch Rickey once said, "Put a rookie on the starting team every year." That simple advice carries huge implications for management succession plans today.

It's critical that business leaders, like chess players, begin to think at least two moves ahead of the competition when it comes to assessing future management talent needs and how to take best advantage of executive recruiters' constant connectivity to the external (and now very global) executive talent market.

Companies need to be prepared to hire groups and lose groups, because that's where recruiting is going.

The World Economic Forum's research has found the United States slipping in terms of its business competitiveness, and countries like Finland, Sweden, Singapore, Switzerland, and Denmark growing or sustaining their competitive edge in the global economy. Although they've had a decided market advantage over other management job candidates throughout much of the history of executive search consulting, U.S. executives may find themselves at some disadvantage in the management talent market of the future because they speak only one language, know only one culture, and have worked in only one country, even if they've had the good fortune to see a bit of the world. Says Paul Sartori, veteran HR leader turned search consultant: "Americans come out of one massive market that they tend to confuse with the rest of the world. By the time they get some international experience, they are in their thirties or forties, or older, while Europeans grow up surrounded by multiple cultures."[12]

Some corporate leadership staffing and development programs are already working against this trend. They are putting business executives with a record of performance in at least two countries, in at least two different functions, and within at least two of the company's different business units on the inside track for their most senior leadership roles. International work assignments—while not without risk to the executive career—may be the strongest predictors of performance and potential within the global operations of the world's largest companies. It is through these postings to foreign business units that corporate ladder climbers, in the words of one senior HR leader, "build the global capabilities they need as leaders."

NOTES

Chapter 1

1. Available online: www.savoypartners.com. Accessed July 11, 2007.
2. Eileen Kamerick, CFO of Heidrick & Struggles, comments to the Americas region conference of the Association of Executive Search Consultants in New York on March 7, 2007, as I reported in ExecuNet's *RecruitSmart Insider* e-newsletter, March 29, 2007.
3. Bush quote sourced from his comments on *The Early Show,* March 12, 2002, during televised tour of his presidential library in College Station, Texas.
4. Romney quote from interview with New England Cable News, April 12, 2002.
5. "Treating Human Capital as an Asset," webinar, Human Capital Institute, November 30, 2006.
6. Susan Hood, "Voice of the Customer: What Do Business Leaders Need from Succession?" remarks at Succession Management Conference, Conference Board, Chicago, October 26, 2006.
7. Saturn Corporation reference is from radio advertisement broadcast on August 18, 2005, which has also appeared on Saturn.com's About Us/Design and Philosophy page.
8. "Bloomberg Careers: Our Strength Lies with Our People," 2005. Available online: www.workthing.com/graphic_profiles/45696/index.html. Accessed July 18, 2007.
9. Steve Lohr, "Cutting Here, but Hiring Over There," *New York Times,* June 24, 2005.
10. For more information on Avery Dennison, see www.AveryDennison.com. Accessed July 18, 2007.

11. J. Terry Schuler, "High-Potential Development: Creating the Right Opportunities for Growth," remarks at Succession Management Conference, Conference Board, Chicago, October 26, 2006.
12. Tanya Clemons, Corporate VP, People and Organization Capability, Microsoft, "Developing and Retaining the Global Leader," remarks to IACPR Conference, New York, October 16, 2006.
13. "The Battle for Brainpower," *Economist,* Oct 5, 2006.
14. "Study Finds Only 25% of Corporations Confident in Executive Bench," press release, RHR International, June 15, 2004, plus personal correspondence.
15. "Effective Recruiting Tied to Stronger Financial Performance," press release, Watson Wyatt Worldwide, August 16, 2005.
16. "Data Establishes Link Between Shareholder Value, and Companies' Ability to Attract, and Retain Top Performers," press release, Hewitt Associates, January 8, 2007. Available online: www.hewittassociates.com/Intl/NA/en-US/AboutHewitt/Newsroom/PressReleaseDetail.aspx?cid=3411. Accessed April 6, 2007.
17. Ernst & Young LLP, ExecuNet, and The Human Capital Institute, "The Aging of the U.S. Workforce: Employer Challenges and Responses," white paper, January 2006.
18. Ernst & Young LLP, ExecuNet, and The Human Capital Institute, "The Aging of the U.S. Workforce."
19. Douglas R. Conant, president and CEO, Campbell Soup Company, "Why Winning in the Workplace Leads to Winning in the Marketplace," keynote address, Talent Management Strategies for Long-Term Success conference, Hunt-Scanlon Advisors, New York, October 19, 2006.
20. Conant, 2006.
21. Peter Drucker, "How to Make People Decisions," *Harvard Business Review,* July 1, 1985. Excerpts available online: www.ezifocus.com/content/thefocus/issue/article.php/article/54300480. Accessed July 18, 2007.
22. Tom Hormby, "Growing Apple with the Macintosh: The Sculley Years," Low End Mac, February 22, 2006. Available online: http://lowendmac.com/orchard/06/0222.html. Access date: July 18, 2007.
23. Thomas J. Neff and James M. Citrin, *You're in Charge—Now What?* (New York: Crown Business, 2005).

Chapter 2

1. Jack Welch, keynote address, Human Capital Advantage Forum, Hunt-Scanlon Advisors, New York, September 25, 2002.
2. "CEO Earnings: 821 Times Minimum-Wage Workers," Reuters, June 30, 2006.

3. Welch, 2002.
4. Christopher Cox, "Speech by SEC Chairman: Remarks Before the Council of Institutional Investors," Washington, DC, March 30, 2006. Available online: www.sec.gov/news/speech/spch033006cc.htm. Accessed January 14, 2008.
5. Cox, 2006.
6. Interview and personal correspondence, April–May 2007.

Chapter 3

1. Roy E. Disney and Stanley P. Gold, "The Mice on Disney's Board," *Los Angeles Times,* March 17, 2005.
2. Patricia Sellers, "Clash of the Corporate Kingmakers," *Fortune,* July 25, 2005.
3. Rakesh Khurana, "Three-Party Exchanges: The Case of Executive Search Firms and CEO Search," Harvard Business School Working Paper, August 2000. Available online: http://ssrn.com/abstract=238608. Accessed July 13, 2007.
4. Bolman, L. G., and Deal, T. E. *Reframing Organizations,* 3rd ed. (San Francisco: Jossey-Bass, 2003). The reference is to structural, political, and cultural and symbolic change frames.
5. "Eisner Gives Disney His Notice," CBS News, September 10, 2004. Available online: www.cbsnews.com/stories/2004/09/10/entertainment/main642482.shtml?source=search_story. Accessed January 14, 2008.
6. Data courtesy of Kennedy Information, Inc., as provided to the author for publication.
7. "Most resources are available . . ." quote is from the late Sidney Boyden, as quoted by Boyden Global Executive Search, which he founded.
8. "Our mission is to contribute . . ." quote sourced from A.T. Kearney Executive Search.
9. "Our clients entrust us . . ." quote sourced from Egon Zehnder International.
10. "When you entrust a firm . . ." quote is sourced from Shepherd, Bueschel & Provus, Inc.
11. Khurana, 2000.

Chapter 4

1. Towers Perrin/CBM, "Recruiting Like Google," E-Document News, n.d. Available online: http://e-documentnews.org/viewmail_edn.cfm?bmailID=373&StoryID=1733&custID=0. Accessed July 14, 2007.
2. "Yahoo to Buy Chinese Search Firm," *USA Today,* Monday, November 24, 2003, Money section.
3. Jim Kennedy, *The Lexicon of Executive Recruiting* (Peterborough, NH: Kennedy Information, 1987).

4. Patricia Sellers, "Clash of the Corporate Kingmakers," *Fortune,* July 11, 2005; Diana Bentley and Andrew Taylor, "In the Headhunters' Sights," *Sunday (London) Times,* May 13, 2007.
5. Oluf C. Jacobsen, *Headhunting: Executive Search* (Schultz, 1985).
6. Plot outline for *Pursued* available online: www.imdb.com/title/tt0385969/. Accessed July 14, 2007.
7. For more on the fictional character Philippa Hunnechurch and her approach to the field, see www.pippahunnechurch.com/headhunting.php. Accessed July 14, 2007.
8. John A. Byrne, *The Headhunters* (New York: Macmillan, 1986).
9. For more on Barbie Adler and her matchmaking service, see www.selective search-inc.com. Accessed July 14, 2007.

Chapter 5

1. James McGregor Burns, *Transforming Leadership: A New Pursuit of Happiness* (New York: Atlantic Monthly Press, 2003), 140.
2. Larry C. Spears, *Mentor Gallery* [Recorded by Gonzaga University, Spokane, Washington].
3. "Courageous Executive Leadership—Critical in Times of Restructuring and Transition," press release, International Association of Corporate & Professional Recruitment (IACPR), August 28, 2004. Available online: www.onrec.com/content2/news.asp?ID=4838. Accessed July 14, 2007.
4. "Nursing Seen as Most Ethical Occupation," *USA Today,* December 12, 2006. Available online: http://www.usatoday.com/printedition/news/20061212/a_honest_chart12.art.htm. Accessed January 14, 2008.
5. "Problems at the Top—Apathy, Contempt for Managers," press release, PR Newswire, January 21, 2005. The press release reported figures based on a survey conducted by Harris Interactive for Age Wave and The Consours Group.
6. "Ford CEO: $28M for 4 months work," CNNMoney.com, April 5, 2007. Available online: http://money.cnn.com/2007/04/05/news/companies/ford_execpay/index.htm?cnn=yes. Accessed July 14, 2007.
7. Rodman L. Drake, "What Makes a Successful Chief Executive?" *Chief Executive,* Spring 1982.
8. Jack Lowe Jr., *Mentor Gallery 2004* [recorded by Gonzaga University, Spokane, Washington, for ORGL 532 section A1 Spring 2006 Module 4: Restorative Justice].
9. Stratford Sherman and Alyssa Freas, "The Wild West of Executive Coaching," *Harvard Business Review,* November 2004.
10. "Outsiders Gaining the Inside Track for CEO Positions," Toronto *Globe and Mail,* October 23, 2006.

11. Greg Farrell, "Mass Exodus by Morgan Stanley Execs Leads to CEO's Resignation," *USA Today,* June 13, 2005.

Chapter 6

1. For Pepsico data, see D. C. McClelland, "Identifying Competencies with the Behavioral Event Interviews," *Psychological Science* 9, no. 5, 1998.
2. For Exxon data, see L. Spencer, "The Economic Value of Emotional Intelligence Competencies and EIC-Based HR Programs," in *The Emotionally Intelligent Workplace: How to Select for, Measure, and Improve Emotional Intelligence in Individuals, Groups, and Organizations,* edited by C. Cherniss and D. Goleman (San Francisco: Jossey-Bass, 2001).

Chapter 7

1. ExecuNet, *2007 Executive Job Market Intelligence Report.* Summary and ordering information available online: www.execunet.com/e_trends_survey.cfm. Accessed July 15, 2007.
2. Corporate Leadership Council, *Shortage Across the Spectrum; The Next Generation; Accelerating the Development of Rising Leaders;* and *Forced Outside: Leadership Talent Sourcing and Retention* (Washington, DC: Advisory Board, 1998). For more information, write to Alexander C. Kleinman at kleinmana@advisory.com.
3. "Leadership IQ Study: Why New Hires Fail," press release, Leadership IQ, September 20, 2005. Available online: www.leadershipiq.com/news_whynewshires fail.html. Accessed July 15, 2007.
4. Laurence J. Stybel, "How to Avoid Stealth Mandates: Advice for Newly Hired/Newly Promoted Leaders," *MIT Sloan Management Review,* Spring 2007.

Chapter 8

1. Peter Bennett, "How to Be a Good Client," shared with the author in private correspondence April 27, 2000. The late Mr. Bennett was principal of Bennett Associates Limited, an executive search firm based in Hong Kong.
2. The quoted passage is from National Association of Boards of Education, "A Board Member's Prayer" (Washington, DC: National Catholic Educational Association, n.d.).
3. HRMAC press release, June 13, 2005.
4. Adapted from Lucien Alziari, "The Successful Search: What Goes on Inside the Corporation," presentation to the IACPR 25th annual conference, New York, October 19, 2003.
5. Peter Felix, letter to the editor, *Executive Recruiter News,* January 2005.
6. Bennett, 2000.

Chapter 9

1. "Women Executives Say Gender Is Still Biggest Hurdle to Career Advancement, Accenture Research Shows," press release, Accenture, March 8, 2007. Available online: http://newsroom.accenture.com. Accessed July 16, 2007.
2. "The Qualities That Distinguish Women Leaders," press release, PRWEB, April 27, 2005. Available online: www.prweb.com/releases/2005/4/prweb233315. htm. Accessed July 16, 2007.
3. Valerie Patterson, "Breaking the Glass Ceiling: What's Holding Women Back?" *CareerJournal.com,* January 13, 1998. Available online: www.careerjournal. com/myc/diversity/19980113-patterson.html. Accessed: July 16, 2007.
4. "For Some Female Executives, It's a Work-Life Imbalance," ExecuNet, Mother's Day ExecuFlash bulletin, May 10, 2001.
5. Catalyst, *2006 Census of Women in Fortune 500 Corporate Officer and Board Positions* (New York: Catalyst, 2007).
6. Norwegian Ministry of Children and Equality, "Gender Distribution in Education and the Workforce," 2007. Available online: www.norway.org/policy/gender/workforce/workforce.htm. Accessed July 16, 2007.
7. Irene Padavic and Barbara Reskin. *Women and Men at Work,* 2nd ed. (Thousand Oaks, CA: Pine Forge Press), pp. 97, 79, 95.
8. Jim Kennedy, *Key Women in Retained Executive Search,* 3rd ed. (Peterborough, NH: Kennedy, 1992).

Chapter 10

1. Patricia Sellers, "Clash of the Corporate Kingmakers," *Fortune,* July 11, 2005. The quote is from Heidrick & Struggles vice chairman Gerard Roche.
2. "ReFAXtions from the LAMP" 18, Summer 1998 (a facsimile publication from the Robert W. Dingman Company).
3. "Headhunting in Corporate America: Clients Are Starting to Ask Embarrassing Questions," cover story, *Forbes,* July 10, 1989

Chapter 11

1. "Nearly Half of U.S. Workers Are Expected to Search for a New Job in 2007," press release, Yahoo! HotJobs, January 3, 2007. Available online: http://yhoo.client.shareholder.com/press/ReleaseDetail.cfm?ReleaseID=224085. Accessed July 17, 2007.
2. Julie Creswell, "Pay Packages Now Allow Executives to Change Jobs with Less Risk," *New York Times,* December 29, 2006.

3. Ernst & Young LLP, ExecuNet, and the Human Capital Institute, "The Aging of the U.S. Workforce: Employer Challenges and Responses," January 2006. Available online: www.maryfurlong.com/studies/AgingWorkforceEYWhitePaper.pdf. Accessed July 17, 2007.
4. Hall & Associates newsletter, Spring 2007.
5. "Former ERE Award Winners Must Innovate Even More in Tight Labor Market," *Inside Recruiting,* October 18, 2006. Available online: www.ere.net/inside-recruiting/news/former-ere-award-winners-must-innovate-179764.asp. Accessed January 14, 2008.
6. American Management Association. *Hiring Costs and Strategies: The AMA Report* (New York: American Management Association, 1986), pp. 1–82. Despite having been conducted more than twenty years ago, the findings of this study remain relevant today.
7. Allan D. R. Stern, opening remarks, National Association of Corporate and Professional Recruiters fifth annual conference, Boston, October 31, 1985. These remarks were published as a guest editorial in *Executive Recruiter News,* November 15, 1985.
8. "To Love, Honor and Provide Career Advice: Survey Finds Spouses Play a Key Role When Evaluating New Job Opportunities," press release, Accountemps, February 12, 2002.
9. "CEO Succession 2005: The Crest of the Turnover Wave," *strategy+business,* Summer 2006.
10. T. K. Kerstetter, "Executive Compensation: Out of Control, or in Line with Today's Talent Realities?", remarks to IACPR Global Conference, New York, October 17, 2006.
11. Chad Terhune, "Recharging Coca-Cola: Recruited from Retirement, Isdell Adds New Fizz to Giant, But Still Faces Big Challenges," *Wall Street Journal,* April 17, 2006. Available online: http://online.wsj.com/public/article/SB114523376275027237-apLj4CLqnqfmZ23_ D1qdmI60t1s_20060425.html?mod=mktw. Accessed January 14, 2008.
12. J. Kevin Day, "What Does It Really Take?" *Pharmaceutical Executive,* August 1, 2005. Available online: www.pharmexec.com/pharmexec/article/articleDetail.jsp?id=175700&pageID=5. Accessed July 17, 2007.

INDEX